Blueprints for Memory

THE TEN MEMORY BLUEPRINTS

1. Initial Letters
2. Six Spaces Around Your Body
3. Rhyming Words
4. Your House
5. The Alphabet
6. The Shoehorn Sentence
7. The Chain
8. The Stack
9. The Cementing Sentence
10. Your Individual Creation

Blueprints
for
Memory

Your Guide
to Remembering
Business Facts, Figures,
and Faces

William D. Hersey

AMERICAN MANAGEMENT ASSOCIATION

This book is available at a special
discount when ordered in bulk quantities.
For information, contact Special Sales Department,
AMACOM, a division of American Management Association,
135 West 50th Street, New York, NY 10020.

Library of Congress Cataloging-in-Publication Data

Hersey, William D.
    Blueprints for memory: your guide to remembering business facts,
figures, and faces / William D. Hersey.
            p.   cm.
      ISBN 0-8144-5961-7
      ISBN 0-8144-7757-7 (pbk.)
      1. Mnemonics.   2. Success in business.   I. Title.
BF385.H455   1989
153.1'4—dc20

                                              89-45452
                                                  CIP

First AMACOM paperback edition 1991.

Printing number

10   9   8   7   6   5   4   3   2   1

I believe there is no one principle which predominates in human nature so much . . . as this passion for superiority.

JOHN ADAMS, 1777

To all who share that conscious passion for superiority and are determined to express the full potential of a fully functioning mind armed with the productive tools of retention, to my wife Fairlee, and to our children, Donna and Glen, this book is dedicated.

Contents

Acknowledgments

There are three individuals who deserve special recognition for their constructive help over a period of many years:

Dr. Morris Young, author of the Foreword, who, many years ago, alerted me to his vast collection of literature on memory improvement and who has been a ready source of encouragement and help ever since.

Teresa Parenti of the Chicago Office of Personnel Management, who introduced me to the vast training network of the U.S. government and provided a productive base for perfecting my ideas.

Judge William Fauver, whose deliberate use of memory methods was a major factor in his career and whose conscientious review of and constructive suggestions on an earlier manuscript contributed to this final version.

THE INDISPENSABLE INGREDIENT

This book would never have been produced if it had not been for the capable, professional editing of my wife, Fairlee, who brought her extensive experience in journalism to bear on every word of this manuscript. Its publication is a testimony to her devotion.

I believe Plato said something to the effect that every man should produce a son, plant a tree, and write a book. We have each played our indispensable part in all three: a son and daughter, many trees, and now this book.

Foreword

Each of us may be regarded as an instrument for a predestined purpose. My first acquaintance with Bill Hersey occurred a quarter century ago when he visited the Morris N. and Chesley V. Young Library of Memory and Mnemonics to browse in our books and minds. His enthusiasm and dedication were boundless. They have continued so, as this brilliant and timely text demonstrates.

Although the mainstream discussion emphasizes techniques for enhancing memory, there is also an overriding sensitiveness to the improvement of personal relationships, particularly in the business world. Methods are presented for keeping up with the information explosion, surviving seminars profitably, and using memory for greater visibility, power, and prestige. These are expressed in terms acceptable to the above-average mind—such as utilizing newspaper headlines as a training device.

Even successful management or sales professionals may sense a need for ways to improve their memory capabilities. An urgency exists for alignment with the memory-machine advantages that are now in the forefront. It's a new game in which leaders cannot afford to mark time.

A principal attraction for aspirants to memory improvment is Hersey's innovative concept of blueprints for the mind. Ten systems of memory aids are organized in that manner, an approach updating what was said to have been invented by Simonides circa 550 B.C.: Objects or ideas can be remembered by imagining places represented by wax writing tablets or sheets of papyrus with lettering on them which are the images of those things.

Memory with respect to foreign languages and numbers is covered in separate chapters, with the supplementary assistance of blueprint principles. Numbers are the language of mathematicians, and in a way they have been treated as a foreign language in relation to methods for recall: In 1634, Pietro Herigon contrived a phonetic numeral system whereby meaningful words could be constructed from a specific sound given to each of the basic numerals to assist memorization. The author's entertaining development of this system in its most current form offers opportunities for rapid acquisition and application.

Preserving his purpose of furthering self-improvement motivations, Bill Hersey frequently inserts sage comments, testimonials, and incisive excerpts to reinforce the acccemptance of what might otherwise seem to be overly burdensome courses of action. Fortunately, the author's personal involvement in the field of memory instruction adds convincing stress to the validity of his recommendations. This becomes apparent in the chapter on remembering names and faces.

Inextricably, the aims and purposes of *Blueprints for Memory* are identified with the fourth of the five divisions of the art of rhetoric: (1) invention, the art of originating or devising; (2) arrangement, or ordering or distributing; (3) style, suitable words and sentences; (4) memory, the firm retention of those words; and (5) delivery, gracefulness of voice, countenance, expressions, and gestures. Appropriately, the author has included a chapter on public speaking.

Bill Hersey has given us an enticingly palatable vehicle for sharpening memory resources, sustaining confidence, weathering the information deluge, and pursuing a more secure path of a positively directed destiny.

MORRIS N. YOUNG, M.D.
Author, *Bibliography of Memory*

1

Memory Basics

In today's dynamic world, businesspeople need at their disposal the most efficient means for processing new information. But, as Tom Peters says in *In Search of Excellence*, "Somewhere along the way to bigness, information overload sets in. Short-term memory can't process it all, or even a small fraction of it, and things get very complicated."[1] As the information explosion pushes into the twenty-first century, businesspeople require the most up-to-date techniques for remembering facts, figures, and faces.

This book assumes that you have a good memory, that at this moment you have stored enough information to keep up with your *present* responsibilities. It is dedicated to helping you achieve a constant increase in your information base by systematically building structures of new knowledge. You will not only learn about methods for reinforcing both the short-term and permanent memory, you will also find—and learn to use—the tools necessary to apply these methods.

BLUEPRINTS FOR MEMORY

The tools used are what I call blueprints for memory. When designing a physical structure such as an office building, the architect prepares hundreds of blueprints showing exactly how every element of the structure is to be completed. Each blueprint is carefully followed, and the entire building takes shape. Once completed, that important capital asset is used for the produc-

1. Thomas J. Peters and Robert H. Waterman, Jr., *In Search of Excellence: Lessons from America's Best Run Companies* (New York: Harper & Row 1982).

1

tive purposes of increasing profit. The blueprints, the visible plans, are forgotten.

Memory blueprints are used to build structures of pertinent knowledge. Just as a book holds information for your eyes to read and your mind to ponder, so memory blueprints hold new information in your mind. You can "look" at this information as often as you need to until it becomes part of your permanent body of knowledge. You can use otherwise unproductive moments to think about and really absorb the new information. This gives you what I call **TNT**.

T otally
N ew
T hinking time

Applied knowledge is power. With these blueprints you will be able to shape the mighty forces of the information age into a powerful propellant for personal advancement and power.

Chapter 2 presents ten blueprints for memory reinforcement. The remaining chapters show you how to apply the blueprints in many aspects of your personal and professional life:

- Remembering names and facts about people
- Self-development
- Goal setting and achievement
- Time management
- Listening
- Business reading
- Seminars
- Sales and persuasion
- Public speaking
- Numbers and data
- Languages

The blueprints are easily grasped. You'll be able to use them immediately to improve your retention of important information and increase your **VIP**.

V isibility
I nfluence
P restige

Your progress in business depends on what you know *and* on the awareness others have of your knowledge. These blueprints will enhance your business personality and status, not just your memory.

Not everyone will need all the methods of memory reinforcement presented in this book. Some work for some people, others fit other people better. We can compare memory to vision. If you cannot read adequately with your natural vision, you reinforce it with glasses prescribed specifically for you. If you have difficulty remembering in certain areas, you can write your own prescription for reinforcing and focusing your most important faculty—your memory.

MEMORY AND ASSOCIATION

We have two types of memory, temporary and permanent. And that's as it should be, or we'd all have dangerously cluttered minds. The temporary memory normally stores about seven items, and the telephone number you just looked up soon evaporates from it. The permanent memory holds information that must be retained. For one reason or another—your natural ability, strong interest, or deliberate repetition, or because the information has

---

YOUR MEMORY *IMPROVES* WITH AGE

As the years roll by, you have more information in your mind. You can use it to form associations with new information as a memory aid. However, when interests change you may forget something you used to be intensely interested in. This often happens with details of completed projects. It also happens to people who have reached a satisfactory level of achievement or whose interests move in other directions. It doesn't mean you are losing your memory.

Memory is the last faculty to go. The first faculty to suffer some diminution is vision, and we immediately use lenses to check the effect of decline. If we use memory methods as lenses to amplify the retentive faculty, it too will function satisfactorily for a long lifetime.

forceful impact or great significance—this information becomes part of the mind's permanent contents.

You can reinforce both the temporary and the permanent memory by using *controlled association*. Think of controlled association as a kind of filing system. You deliberately associate new information with something you already know, and mentally link them. Then you can extract the new data from your mental file cabinet, because you know what "file" to look in. The ten memory blueprints presented in this book apply controlled association to both temporary and permanent memory.

The relationship of temporary memory to permanent memory may be likened to a sponge and a bucket. When a sponge is oversaturated, some of the liquid in it starts to drain out and evaporate. However, by squeezing the liquid into a bucket, you can save it and then use the sponge over and over again to save up more bucketfuls. Reinforcing the temporary memory by controlled association, you can grasp new information and, with frequent repetition, "squeeze" its contents into the bucket of the permanent memory.

We build a body of knowledge the way we build our physical bodies. When we chew food enough to permit it to be swallowed, we have done all we can to aid its digestion. After that, the process is automatic. The body digests the food and distributes its nutrients to the places necessary for growth and dependable strength. Similarly, if we "chew" information sufficiently— that is, review and repeat it—the mental digestive process will automatically make that information part of our structure of thought.

We can't eat a week's worth of meals on a Sunday. The food must be divided into meals, and each one must be chewed adequately. Similarly, we cannot cram too much information into the mind at one time and expect it to become permanent. It must be divided into mental meals and each one reviewed, "chewed," for effective mental digestion.

After thoroughly absorbing knowledge by association, we reach the stage of cognition. At this point we know a subject so thoroughly that it is instantly available. We don't have to stop and consciously think about it. It's in our direct-access memory. This is true of most of the knowledge we use every day.

MEMORY AS AN AID TO LEARNING

There are six steps to the learning process: motivation, organization, concentration, thinking about new information, repetition and review, and cognition. When you use the ten memory blueprints, you'll find each of these steps easier.

1. Your *motivation* will increase because the blueprints make it easy to learn information.
2. These blueprints for memory make it possible to *organize* any type of information, just as a filing system enables you to collect information from an organized source.
3. Your *concentration* is enhanced because the blueprints give your mind a track to run on.
4. These blueprints hold information as a complete unit in your mind so that you can *think about the new information* and be certain that you are aware of every aspect of it as you build your structure of knowledge: your permanent memory.
5. If you can *repeat and review* information at intervals, you will remember it more easily and quickly than if you try to cram it in all at once.
6. Spaced repetition brings the information to the *cognitive* level, where it becomes part of the permanent structure of useful knowledge. In this final step, new information can be used automatically, without conscious thought.

Whatever you need to remember or learn, no matter how extensive, can be mastered by using memory blueprints. Focus on what you want and need to remember and now have difficulty remembering. If you tailor these methods to your own requirements, you will soon see swift progress toward your goals.

Come fill your lamp with **OIL** and let

    O   rganized
    I   nformation
    L   ead the way!

2

Ten Memory Blueprints

We have all used memory joggers to remember necessary information. You may have learned two classics in childhood from your music teacher. Remember **FACE** and Every Good **B**oy **D**oes **F**ine? These two memory joggers were introduced to help you remember the spaces and lines on the musical staff. The words themselves have nothing to do with music, of course. But **FACE**, which uses letters to form a memorable word, and Every Good **B**oy **D**oes **F**ine, a memorable sentence composed of words beginning with the important five letters, are an effective technique for "storing" the parts of the musical staff until they become second nature to you.

Here's another example: The authors of *In Search of Excellence*[1] realized the need to make abstract information memorable. They developed terms for seven management styles, each beginning with the letter *s*. Then they designed a framework for the seven styles, using circles connected with lines. It resembles a molecule. It's a simple way to think about managing, and the concept caught on quickly. Students grasped the principles so easily that a leading professor of management said that it took all the mystery out of teaching the subject! This is powerful testimony to the value of arranging information in easily remembered form for concentrated, constructive thinking.

Ten memory blueprints are introduced in this chapter. The blueprints are plans that can help you build new information into a sound structure of knowledge. You'll see them applied in later chapters. Not all the blueprints are equally effective for everyone. Try them all to determine which ones will serve you best.

1. Thomas J. Peters and Robert H. Waterman, Jr., *In Search of Excellence: Lessons from America's Best Run Companies* (New York: Harper & Row, 1982).

MEMORY BLUEPRINT 1: INITIAL LETTERS

The first blueprint consists of a memorable word or phrase, using the first letters of the items you want to remember. You start by writing down the ideas you need to remember and isolating the key word or phrase in each; then you take the first letters of all the key words and spell a word or phrase.

To illustrate, we'll practice remembering six rules for personal empowerment. Because this is your first exercise, and because this blueprint is used so frequently, I'll describe the process in some detail.

First, here are the rules:

1. Listen; people respect and reward good listeners.
2. Show an interest in others.
3. Smile.
4. Encourage them to talk.
5. Make them feel important.
6. Use their name; it's a tribute to personal identity.

Now, choose the key words in each item.

1. *Listen;* people respect and reward good listeners.
2. Show an *interest* in others.
3. *Smile.*
4. Encourage them to *talk.*
5. Make them feel *important.*
6. Use their *name;* it's a tribute to personal identity.

The first letters of the key word in each rule form the blueprint.

L isten
I nterest
S mile
T alk
I mportant
N ame

You have just formed the two-word memory jogger **LIST IN.**
These two words will help you remember the six rules of empowerment. Using Memory Blueprint 1, you add the rules to
your temporary memory; then, by repetition, you gradually
transfer them to your permanent memory.

Sometimes the letters in their original sequence just don't add
up to anything. If it's not critical to remember the items in any
particular order, try rearranging the list so that you can create a
recognizable word.

Let's say, for instance, that you're a real estate agent, and you
have planned an open house for one of your listings for tomorrow afternoon. You know your morning will be completely taken
up with meetings, so you must be able to keep the last-minute
details in your head. You want to make sure you remember to
bring the information handouts, that you have a good supply of
business cards, that you put up directional signs at key intersec-
tions, that you pack everything you need for the hospitality table, and that you bring the report of the termite inspection.

Your mental list looks like this:

> **I** nformation sheets
> **C** ards
> **D** irectional signs
> **H** ospitality table
> **T** ermite report

Rearrange to **DITCH,** and you've got a quick memory jogger!

MEMORY BLUEPRINT 2:
SIX SPACES AROUND YOUR BODY

Memory Blueprint 2 uses six spaces around your body—to your
left, in front of you, to your right, in back of you, under your
feet, and on top of your head—for remembering six headlines.

Since headlines express the key element in every news story,
your practice in memorizing them can be readily transferred to
remembering other key points in whatever material you are tack-
ling.

As key words, headlines let you recall the context and content of the stories or main points in a speech or conference.

Here's how Memory Blueprint 2 works using headlines from newspapers. Start with this list of six headline words:

1. *fire*
2. *oil*
3. *accident*
4. *murder*
5. *snow*
6. *food*

Think of the following headlines as *pictures*, and mentally place each in one of those spaces around your body. First visualize a fire and put it to your left; make it big. Make a picture about oil and place it vividly in front of you. To your right picture an accident. Quick, now: What is to your left? In front? To your right? Great! Next, in back of you picture a murder. Under your feet see snow. On your head visualize food. Always make your pictures vivid and as personal as possible. Recall again. What is to your left? In front? To your right? Behind you? Under your feet? On your head?

I'm sure these pictures came readily to mind. Why? Because you did two things: You made a picture of something you wanted to remember, and you put that picture in a definite place for ready review.

By associating pictures of something you want to remember—these words—with locations that you can easily recall in order, you can store any information systematically. It will be at your instant command. This is controlled association, the mental filing system introduced in Chapter 1.

MEMORY BLUEPRINT 3:
WORDS THAT RHYME WITH NUMBERS

This third blueprint is particularly valuable when you want to remember something *in a definite order*. We are used to filing or associating material numerically: order numbers, route numbers,

RHYMING WORDS

Ed Foreman, president of Executive Development Systems in Dallas, Texas, has conducted his "Successful Life Course" for many years. You may have seen him on *Sixty Minutes*. Ed knows that repetition is essential for implanting a new attitude in the habitual thought patterns of the mind.

He uses Memory Blueprint 3 (Rhyming Words) to help people remember the twelve basic habit patterns of a winner.

1. *[Run]* Don't condemn, criticize, or complain. Think of ways to improve the situation. The big rewards come to those who find the solution, not the difficulty.
2. *[Zoo]* Show honest and heartfelt appreciation. Let others know they are involved.
3. *[Tree]* Think good thoughts about other people and yourself.
4. *[Door]* Give before you get. Always give others a reason to agree with you before asking them.
5. *[Bee hive]* Smile often. It generates enthusiasm, friendliness, and good will.
6. *[Sick]* Remember names. A person's name is the sweetest, most important sound he hears; it instantly captures his attention each time it is used.
7. *[Heaven]* Be an effective communicator by listening. Encourage others to talk about themselves by asking questions: when, where, who, what, how, why?
8. *[Gate]* Think, act, and look happy and successful, and you will begin to *feel* and *become* happy and successful.
9. *[Wine]* Never engage in worry conversations or participate in group gossip sessions.
10. *[Den]* Always greet others with a positive, cheerful statement, not with "How are you?"
11. *[Football eleven]* When someone asks, "How are you?" answer with an enthusiastic *"Terrific!"*
12. *[Shelf]* Look for and expect good things to happen to you. Ask others, "What good things are happening to you today?"

dates, and steps in professional procedures. Memory Blueprint 3 uses a series of specific nouns—picture words—that rhyme with the words for the numbers one through ten. The method is to picture information and link it with a series of pictures representing something you already know—numbers.

One sounds like "gun." Picture a gun.
Two sounds like "shoe." Picture a shoe.
Three sounds like "tree." Picture a tree.
Four sounds like a "door." Picture a door.
Five sounds like "dive." Picture a dive.
Six sounds like "sticks." Picture sticks.
Seven sounds like "heaven." Picture heaven.
Eight sounds like "gate." Picture a gate.
Nine sounds like "wine." Picture wine.
Ten sounds like "hen." Picture a hen.

Now you can use this ten-point blueprint to remember ten ideas, say in a speech, by associating each one with a numbered picture. Here are ten ideas:

1. Unemployment
2. Health
3. Housing
4. Inflation
5. Cost of living
6. Education
7. Crime
8. Defense
9. Budget
10. Welfare

First, visualize unemployment and associate it vividly with *gun.* Next, picture health and associate it vigorously with shoe; picture housing and associate it vividly with *tree;* now review your pictures for *gun, shoe,* and *tree,* and see how quickly they bring the first three ideas to mind.

Let's do three more: Picture inflation with *door.* Picture cost of living with *dive.* Picture education with *sticks.* Be sure to make the pictures active, and involve yourself. Now review the first six to be certain that you have firmly attached your pictures representing ideas from the speech to the pictures representing numbers. If one association is weak, strengthen it by further intensification or exaggeration. Remember, the association doesn't have to be logical; sometimes the more ridiculous, the better.

Down the homestretch: Associate crime with *heaven*, defense with *gate*, budget with *wine*, and welfare with *hen*. Then review all ten points. You will prove to yourself that pictures persist and that you will remember what you thought you could not.

You have now demonstrated to yourself that you can file ideas mentally and pictorially and then *re*collect information from that file. So far, you have used three purposeful blueprints or patterns for organizing and processing information: Memory Blueprint 1 uses initial letters; Memory Blueprint 2, the spaces around your body; and Memory Blueprint 3, rhyming words with numbers.

MEMORY BLUEPRINT 4: YOUR HOUSE

The house blueprint is one of the most efficient blueprint forms—and one of the oldest. About 450 B.C., the Greek poet Simonides often entertained at the homes of influential people. One night he had just left a banquet hall when the ceiling fell in, killing everyone inside. Simonides was able to identify the bodies because he was able to remember where each person had been sitting. This developed into the technique of using rooms as storage places for *mental images*.

More than 300 years later, the great Roman orator Cicero pictured a series of objects in and around his dwelling to remember the key points of his orations. This was his memory blueprint. When he was speaking to the senate, he never missed a point; he said exactly what he had planned to say. Furthermore, he persuaded his listeners! Cicero called memory the golden goddess. If you've ever left a conference or a sales interview and realized afterward that you had omitted something you had planned to say, take a lesson from Cicero.

You can easily adapt Cicero's system to your own house. I'll show you how, using my house as an example.

I'll start with my kitchen, since it is the first room I enter. I select:

1. Sink
2. Stove
3. Chair

4. Table
5. Refrigerator

Passing into the living room, I choose:

6. Rug
7. Easy chair
8. TV
9. Lamp
10. Window

In the bathroom I select:

11. Tub
12. Washbasin
13. Medicine cabinet
14. Mirror
15. Towel rack

In the bedroom I choose:

16. Bed
17. Bureau
18. Closet
19. Night table
20. Alarm clock

THE SINS OF SALVATORE D'AMATO

There is a tombstone in Florence, Italy, with this inscription:

Here lies Salvatore D'Amato
May God pardon his sins.
1312

What were his sins? He invented the simple optical lens! People at the time said that if God had wanted people to have better vision, he would have given it to them. But this simple lens has enabled untold millions to read when normal vision fades. Similarly, *simple* methods of retention can amplify and focus retentive power—memory power—to meet most of our realistic needs for remembering.

Now we'll use these locations to remember twenty key words
from headlines in *The Wall Street Journal*. After that you'll create
your own house list and remember twenty more words. The
twenty *Journal* headline words are:

shipwreck	*Russians*
children	*tornado*
dollar	*fire*
President	*blood*
bananas	*convicts*
ambassador	*gold*
drugs	*robbery*
France	*flood*
baseball	*bomb*
space shuttle	*hijacking*

See yourself walking into the kitchen. Put a picture of a ship-
wreck in the kitchen sink. Put your picture for children on the
stove. Picture the dollar on the kitchen chair; the President on
the table; bananas in the refrigerator.

Now: What's in the sink? On the stove? On the chair? On the
table? In the refrigerator? If you missed any, make the pictures
more vivid. It is the clarity of your involvement in them that
prevents forgetting.

Continue with the next room. Picture an ambassador on the
living-room rug. In the easy chair, put your picture for drugs;
on the TV screen, see a vivid picture that to you means France;
with the reading lamp, baseball; in the window, a space shuttle.

Check: What's on the sink? Stove? Chair? Table? Refrigerator?
Rug? Easy chair? TV? Lamp? Window? I'll bet you remembered
them all.

You've already memorized ten headline words. Let's do ten
more: In the bathtub are Russians; in the washbasin, a tornado;
in the medicine cabinet, a fire. Remember, make these pictures
impressive. On the mirror is blood; with the towel rack are con-
victs.

Check again: What's in the tub? Washbasin? Medicine cabinet?
Mirror? Towel rack? I'm sure you remembered every one!

Let's enter the bedroom. On the bed, gold; on the bureau, robbery; in the closet, a flood; on your night table, a bomb; with your alarm clock, hijacking.

Now let's check out the entire house. What do you associate with each of these: Sink? Stove? Chair? Table? Refrigerator? Rug? Easy chair? TV? Lamp? Window? Tub? Washbasin? Medicine cabinet? Mirror? Towel rack? Bed? Bureau? Closet? Night table? Alarm clock?

I assume you've done well on this because the beauty of the checking system is that you learn instantly what has been forgotten. You then can visualize it more vividly for better memorizing.

Creating your list to fit your own home is truly magnetic for your memory; you are working with objects that are very familiar to you and that you are personally involved with. When you put something on an object in your own house, you add memory magnetism that you get nowhere else.

Now create your own personal memory path through your own home. Don't use more than four rooms, and don't select more than five items in each room. The exercise should take about seven minutes.

First Room

1. _____

2. _____

3. _____

4. _____

5. _____

Second Room

6. _____

7. _____

8. _____

9. _____

10. _____

Third Room

11. _____

12. _____

13. _____

14. _____

15. _____

Fourth Room

16. _____

17. _____

18. _____

19. _____

20. _____

I keep emphasizing "your *own* picture," because it is the real key to a better memory. Trust the picture you think of; you don't have to explain it to anyone. Your pictures will involve personal situations, emotions, humor—all of which add memory magnetism.

Make your picture for each of the following headline words from *The Wall Street Journal,* or select words from the newspaper of your choice. Place each one in order on the objects you selected. Review one room at a time before continuing to the next. Don't worry if you miss one or two items.

First Room

  oil

  Brazil

the dollar
American Airlines
Congress

Second Room

White House
Big Board
CBS
raft
broadcasting

Third Room

terrorist
Paris
troops
the President
Chinese

Fourth Room

governors
microcomputer
Soviet officials
Chrysler
Chicago

Now let me illustrate how I was able to use Memory Blueprint 4 to remember the first ten points I heard in a talk on Latin America given by a well-known journalist.

His first point was that the media had not been paying much attention to Latin America: I pictured myself at my kitchen sink sponging Latin America off the front page of a newspaper. His second point was that the United States would have to pay more attention to Latin America: I pictured Uncle Sam tending a Latin American kettle on my stove.

Then, point three, he discussed the problem of rising expectations in Latin America: I pictured a Latin American gentleman standing on my kitchen chair while a flood of rising expectations swirled up around him. The fourth was about the frustrations in dealing with Latin America: I pictured Uncle Sam and a Latin American glaring at each other across my table.

As his fifth point, the journalist indicated that there was still hope for Latin America: I pictured Bob Hope in my refrigerator. His sixth point was that Latin America was not divorced from the rest of the world: I pictured Latin America on a map on one side of my living-room rug and the world on the other.

The seventh point was made as an incidental remark; he had been talking with several Latin American editors who thought some of our well-publicized problems were evidence of our strength: I pictured these editors all sitting in my easy chair. The eighth point was that there were certain restrictions in dealing with Latin America: I pictured Latin Americans tying up some-one on my TV.

The ninth point was the conservatism of Latin Americans as an obstacle: I pictured a well-known conservative holding up my reading lamp like a torch. Finally, point ten, he referred to the population explosion: I pictured millions of people standing out-side my window.

I suspect that some of my associations in memorizing those ten points seem strange. I've described them to illustrate to you how individualized, personal, and even illogical they can be. Use whatever works.

You can improve the efficiency of your memory in just five minutes of daily practice with your own house memory blue-print. Refer to the list of objects in your house as necessary, but you'll know it cold after a couple of days. Practice each day for five days with twenty different headlines. Pretty soon you'll be convinced that *anything* can be visualized on any object in your house. Each day's headlines will drop out as you do the next day's, since your mind will recognize this as just a warm-up ex-ercise.

For your further practice, memorize twenty headlines from the second and third columns of the front page of *The Wall Street Journal* or possibly the table of contents of a current issue of *Time, Newsweek, Fortune,* or whatever would be most useful for you in your business.

The information explosion highlights the immense value of us-ing the tools of controlled association. Remember my promise:

Practice with twenty words five minutes a day for five days; with a total of only twenty-five minutes you will develop a memory skill you can depend on for the rest of your life.

MEMORY BLUEPRINT 5: THE ALPHABET

The alphabet is the basis for another easily remembered blueprint. With it, you can quickly remember a long list of items in exact sequence. Here's how it works: Each letter of the alphabet is assigned a word that starts with that letter. Then you create a visual image based on that word in conjunction with the point you want to remember.

The trick is that each "cue" word is short and, as much as possible, represents the sound of the letter. For instance, in my list, *a* is "ape" and *b* is "bee."

Here is an example of how this might be used to remember six steps in a management formula, which, if continually applied by executives and supervisors, will provide for the observance of basic principles of management. Here is the formula as developed by Lawrence A. Apply, former head of the American Management Association.

A Management Formula

which if continuously applied by executives and supervisors, will provide for the observance of basic principles of management:

I. ORGANIZATION CLARIFICATION
   1. Functions to be performed
   2. Authority to go with functions
   3. Relationships with others

II. STANDARDS OF PERFORMANCE
   1. Conditions that will exist when functions are satisfactorily performed

III. PERFORMANCE REVIEW
   1. Periodic comparison of complete individual performance with the standards

IV. HELP AND INFORMATION
1. Material, instruction, advice, guidance, or contacts required to correct individual or group weaknesses in performance, skill, knowledge, habits, or attitudes

V. SOURCE (of help and information)
1. Immediate supervisor
2. Company specialist
3. Outside specialist to be brought in
4. Outside institution of learning

VI. TIME SCHEDULE
1. For individuals
2. For groups (meetings, conferences, councils, classes, etc.)

Here's how you might apply the alphabet to remembering the six principle steps. The pictorial associations are mine. Yours will be different. Try yours.

A*pe:* "organization clarification." I pictured an **APE** drawing an organization chart.

B*ee:* "standards of performance." I owned a beehive once, and so for this I pictured examining **BEES** as they came back to the hive to see how well they had performed.

C*edar:* "performance review." I cut forty **CEDAR** posts on my property, and I pictured my wife reviewing my performance.

D*eed:* "help and information." I pictured an attorney helping me clear the **DEED** to the adjoining property.

E*el:* "source (of help and information)." I remembered and pictured that the source of every **EEL** in the world is said to be the Saragossa Sea.

F*ox:* "time schedule." I pictured a **FOX** with a stopwatch.

The words I have found most useful for the rest of the alphabet are:

G	*golf*
H	*H-bomb*
I	*eye*
J	*bluejay*
K	*cake*

L	hell
M	ham
N	hen
O	a big *O*
P	peas
Q	cucumber
R	hair
S	*s*-curve
T	tea
U	ewe or *u*-turn
V	victory
W	double yolk
X	axe
Y	yo-yo
Z	zebra

This alphabetical blueprint gives you an excellent opportunity to express your individuality. Whether your interest is in animals, jewelry, food, or the military, you can create alphabetical lists based on it. You're limited only by your imagination.

MEMORY BLUEPRINT 6: THE SHOEHORN SENTENCE

Just as a shoehorn helps you slip your foot into your shoe, the shoehorn sentence eases new information into your mind even though the sentence itself may have no logical connection with the subject. It's a great blueprint for remembering a procedure that consists of a series of steps that have to be done in a particular order.

It works like this: The first letter of each key word becomes the first letter of *another* word; all the substitute words, in sequence, make a memorable sentence—whimsical, maybe, but memorable.

As an example, navigators use a shoehorn sentence to remember these five points in setting a compass: compass, deviation, magnetic, variation, and true. The initials **C**, **D**, **M**, **V**, and **T** are turned into **Can Dead Men Vote Twice?**

Here are the initials to the steps in a certain professional procedure. Before looking to see what the procedure is, create a seven-word shoehorn sentence to help you remember these initials in order.

L _____

S _____

C _____

Q _____

A _____

C _____

C _____.

Have you composed a sentence? Now I'll tell you what the procedure is: a seven-step process, recommended by a great sales trainer, J. Douglas Edwards, for handling a customer's final objection. The seven steps—which *must* be done in order—are:

1. Listen.
2. Sell.
3. Confirm.
4. Question.
5. Answer.
6. Confirm.
7. Close.

The shoehorn sentence doesn't have to be logical—just memorable. Your sentence might be somewhat related, such as Listen Sincerely, Closely Question, And Collect Cash. A woman in South Carolina came up with this one: Love Some Chick Quietly After Church Closes.

MEMORY BLUEPRINT 7: THE CHAIN

The chain blueprint connects, or chains, the picture of one item to a previous one. Say someone has mentioned six stocks to you:

Armco Steel, General Foods, Telstar, Texaco, Consolidated Edison, and MGM. Conjure up a picture for each and create a pictorial or narrative chain that connects them in a row.

I would picture Armco Steel as a knight in armor serving
Wheaties to people on a satellite bearing the Texaco star and
landing on Consolidated Edison's property guarded by the MGM
lion. It's a fast-moving linkage that will deliver one picture after
another to your memory.

This blueprint is good for remembering temporary lists and for
listening in high-speed situations.

MEMORY BLUEPRINT 8: THE STACK

The stack blueprint is similar to Memory Blueprint 7, but instead
of linking pictures together as a chain you visualize them stacked
one on top of the other. For instance, your picture of Wheaties
will rest on top of the knight, who will be on top of the satellite,
and so on.

A young woman I know once found herself in the elevator
with the vice-president of the company where she had just been
hired as a summer intern. During their short conversation, the
vice-president mentioned four managers he thought she should
meet: Paul Spires in Long-Range Planning, Martha Appleton in
Marketing, Dave Stein in New-Product Development, and Alice
Bettleton in Finance. She couldn't write the names down while
in the elevator, but she knew she had better remember them! So
she built this stack:

> **ALICE BET** a **TON** with *company money* (FINANCE); she reached
> up and put her winnings in the *newly designed* (NEW-PRODUCT
> DEVELOPMENT) beer **STEIN; MARTHA** took the money to the
> *market* to buy **APPLES;** while **PAUL** climbed up to the top of
> the **SPIRE** so he could see far into the *distance* (LONG-RANGE
> PLANNING) and watch where she went.

MEMORY BLUEPRINT 9: THE CEMENTING SENTENCE

If you are a person who thinks verbally rather than pictorially,
use the cementing sentence to construct a sentence made up of

the key words you want to remember. Remember the key words from the rules of personal empowerment shown at the beginning of this chapter: *"listen," "interest," "smile," "talk," "important," "name"*? You might create a cementing sentence like this: **LISTEN** with **INTEREST, SMILE, TALK,** and use **IMPORTANT NAMES.** Or, a slight variation: Suppose your husband calls you just as you're leaving the office and asks you to pick up some milk, sugar, bread, scallions, and mushrooms. To keep the list in your mind, make up this sentence and say it over and over to yourself as you're driving home:

I am mixing **MILK** and **SUGAR,** spreading it on **BREAD** to make a sandwich of **SCALLIONS** and **MUSHROOMS.**

MEMORY BLUEPRINT 10: INDIVIDUAL CREATION

Determine which of these nine blueprints serve you best in organizing the important information you must retain. Practice them with headline words every day until you are thoroughly familiar with their use. Then create your own blueprint, using your personal interests. If you are interested in baseball, use the nine player positions. If you play golf, you have eighteen tees, traps, and holes. If you bowl, think of what you encounter there: shoes, ball, towel, balk line, gutter, alley, strike, spare, rack, score sheet. Since your blueprint is built around an activity that is familiar to you, it will be easy to remember. Pleasurable and personal associations automatically add impact.

PRACTICE, PRACTICE, PRACTICE

Imagination is the glue that holds ideas together. Like glue, it requires some "setting" time to make a permanent bond. Based on my experience with business-related information, the more reviews and repetitions you can manage, the better, but a dozen spaced reviews are a good starting point.

You may be wondering where you'll find time for practice sessions. Actually, it's easier than you think. There are many opportunities for purposeful repetition every day. Here are a few suggestions:

Morning

  Upon awakening
  Jogging
  Walking
  Bicycling
  Exercising

Commuting

  Driving
  Red lights
  Commercials on car radio
  Rhythm of wiper blades
  Rhythm of train wheels
  Subway noises

At the Office

  Waiting, especially on the telephone
  Afternoon slump
  Riding in the elevator
  Making photocopies

Lunch Break

  In line at the bank
  Waiting for your meal
  Walk in the park

TV Prime Time

  Commercials—prime time for *your* affirmations

Night

  Before going to sleep
  When awake during the night, in time to your heartbeat
  Blocking out annoying night noises such as dogs barking or
    neighbors' loud music

GENERATING MENTAL POWER

We don't generate electricity. We simply whirl magnets through the existing field of electrical force and collect the electricity into useful form. Similarly, we can circulate memory blueprints through a field of knowledge and collect information into a useful form.

SUMMARY

Now let's recap the ten types of blueprints. Chapter 3 shows you how to apply them to various aspects of self-improvement and goal attainment.

The Ten Memory Blueprints

1. Initial letters
2. Six spaces around your body
3. Rhyming words
4. Your house
5. The alphabet
6. The shoehorn sentence
7. The chain
8. The stack
9. The cementing sentence
10. Your individual creation

Remember, you may not need all these blueprints. Their purpose is to give you

T *otally*
N *ew*
T *hinking time*

and

V *isibility*
I *nfluence*
P *restige*

3

Memory: The Golden Key to Self-Improvement

Continuous learning is the imperative of the present. Ongoing self-improvement no longer refers to whatever you'd like to study for "enrichment," but to what you *must* do to keep from going broke when the skills you thought would sustain you for a lifetime just aren't enough.

Marina N. Whitman, vice-president of General Motors' public affairs staff, says, "An assumption that's already fallen by the wayside is the idea that education and training acquired by people in their teens or twenties are sufficient for a lifetime."

Since your attitude is vital to success in any self-improvement program you undertake, let's consider the impact of your self-image and make certain it will be a dependable ally in your determination to develop your full potential.

Let's test your present thinking about yourself, starting with something that is uniquely yours: your name. Your name, your identity, is a key to your self-image; it can either help or hinder any plan you have for self-improvement. Consider that in the first sixteen years of your life your name was often used negatively: "Bobby, eat your cereal!" "Debbie, don't touch that!" "Johnny, don't *do* that!" "Sally, why can't you pick up your room?" "Eric, if I've told you once, I've told you a thousand times! . . ." And so on . . . *always with your name*. It has been estimated that parents and other authority figures use about twenty-five negative statements to every positive one. Unfortunately, most of the negative statements are injected with the "needle" of a person's name.

What is your name? What is your self-image? Describe yourself in words, each one beginning with a letter in your first name. Write the descriptive words in order on the following lines.

———	————————————————————
———	————————————————————
———	————————————————————
———	————————————————————
———	————————————————————
———	————————————————————
———	————————————————————

How many of the words you selected were positive? How many were negative or self-deprecating? If all your self-descriptive words were positive, you are already a winner. On the other hand, if some were negative, you can reverse them and reprogram your self-image. Your best efforts to change your life or habits will have only temporary success unless you reprogram your self-image. When your self-image has become positive, all systems are "go."

REPROGRAMMING YOUR SELF-IMAGE

You can use your memory to make your subconscious a purposeful partner in building and maintaining your desired self-image, rooting out and removing hidden obstacles, breaking bad habits, and achieving every desirable goal. You have a right to be everything your conscious mind wants you to be.

Use your memory blueprints in combination with the following three steps for reprogramming your self-image:

Step 1: Redescribe Yourself in Positive Terms. Using Memory Blueprint 1 and the letters in your first name, build a new, positive concept of your self-image. For example, take someone named Robert. He might say in positive terms, "I am Robert! I am:

> "**R** esourceful,
> "**O** ptimistic,
> "**B** rilliant,
> "**E** nergetic,
> "**R** eliable,
> "**T** errific."

Sheila could say, "I am Sheila. I am:

> "**S** uccessful,
> "**H** elpful,
> "**E** nergetic,
> "**I** ntelligent,
> "**L** imitless,
> "**A** ctive."

Craig could say, "I am:

> "**C** reative,
> "**R** eliable,
> "**A** ctive,
> "**I** ntelligent,
> "**G** reat."

Now take *your* name and write down positive words after each letter. Memorize the words and repeat them as often as possible. Each review takes only a few seconds.

To stimulate your thinking, here is the full alphabet with several positive words and a negative word for each letter. Which will you choose to be?

A ctive, alert, affirmative, *or* . . . . apathetic
B right, building, balanced, *or* . . . . blocking
C ompetent, constructive, confident, *or* . . . . cringing
D etermined, dynamic, definite, *or* . . . . despairing
E nergetic, enthusiastic, expansive, *or* . . . . expendable
F uture-focused, friendly, functioning, *or* . . . . failing
G oing forward, great, gaining, *or* . . . . giving up
H elpful and healthy, *or* . . . . heckling

I ntelligent, important, interesting, *or* . . . . indifferent
J udicious and joyous, *or* . . . . a jerk
K een, knowledgeable, kind, *or* . . . . a killjoy
L imitless, lively, living it up, *or* . . . . lying low
M ighty, making the most of moments,
    or . . . . minimizing your mind
N imble, noble, and noteworthy, *or* . . . . negative
O ptimistic, organized, open-minded, *or* . . . . obstructive
P ositive, purposeful, persistent, *or* . . . . precarious
Q ualified, quick, quiet, *or* . . . . a quitter
R esourceful, reliable, responsible, ready, *or* . . . . . retreating
S trong, successful, sensational, *or* . . . . a sluggard
T errific, triumphant, tremendous, *or* . . . . trailing
U nshakable, unconquerable, understanding,
    or . . . . unfortunate
V igorous, victorious, vital, and vibrant, *or* . . . . . vanquished
W armhearted, wonderful, worthy, *or* . . . . washed up
X ceptional, *or* . . . . x'd out
Y outhful, young in mind, *or* . . . . just yearning
Z ealous, zipping ahead, zestful, *or* . . . . zilch

The choices are up to you.

In the Scriptures and in literature **I AM** has been used to reinforce the sense of basic, essential identity. You can use it for the
same purpose. When someone asks, "Who are you?" or "What
is your name?" most of us answer by saying, "I am . . ." followed by our name. For a self-improvement boost, use the letters in **I AM** as positive starters. For example:

> **I** ntelligent
> **A** ctive
> **M** ind

or

> **I** nspirational
> **A** ble
> **M** anager

If you're feeling low, or if someone's words or actions have put you down, here's a quick remedy. Say to yourself, "That's her problem. I am . . ."; then state your name and go down the list of your chosen positive words. This mental exercise will wash away any negatives from your mind. Your positive memory jogger based on your name is an instant antidote for mental poison.

Step 2: Visualize and Personalize. For every aspect of your life, visualize each of the positive words connected with the letters of your first name. For instance Robert has the word *resourceful* in his name. He can declare, "I am resourceful, mentally and physically"—and then visualize himself solving a complex problem at work or successfully improvising during a home-repair job. Sheila, whenever she feels particularly dejected, can run through her self-identity words and see some heartwarming pictures of herself:

- *Successfully* chairing the United Way campaign at her office
- *Helping* a neighbor's daughter with her math assignment
- Feeling *energetic* after a tough game of tennis
- Being complimented for her *intelligent* presentation
- Constructing a *limitless* list of options
- *Actively* involved in church and community activities

Do this with all the qualities you want to express and reinforce. Make strong and very specific images. Don't merely say to yourself, "I am competent." Actually *see* yourself at the conference table briefing senior management on your manufacturing proposal. Think of this exercise as watching home movies of yourself at your best. It will be a bulwark against negative suggestions you encounter daily, such as the television commercials that insist, "You have problems sleeping, digesting food, pleasing your family, . . ." Silence these suggestions and treat yourself to a new and brighter view of your identity with the positive power of your name.

Step 3: Repeat and Repeat. To correct hidden negatives, forceful repetition is needed. After all, it took you a long time to develop those negative ideas about yourself; you won't get rid of them in just one recitation of positive qualities. There are four easy, natural ways to work in the practice you need and establish a habitual pattern of repetition. They are encompassed in the words "sleep," "walk," "heart," and "jog." Using Memory Blueprint 9, create a sentence to cement the ideas: "While I'm sleepwalking my heart's jogging."

1. *Sleep.* Just before you fall asleep, reverse the vague negative suggestions of your subconscious mind by repeating the positive qualities you've identified in your name.

2. *Walk.* You can invite your new self-image to walk with you and establish a permanent, productive, and powerful relationship. While walking, practice saying the positive words in time with your steps. You'll be surprised how soon it will become effortless and how soon you'll feel an underlying confidence that will reshape your self-image even when you are not consciously aware of it.

3. *Heart.* There is a natural inner relationship, a sympathetic vibration, between the rhythm of your heart and that of your mind. Use your heartbeat as another vehicle for constant repetition.

4. *Jog.* Do you jog? Why not jog your self-image for a positive mental result? You can repeat the positive words based on your name with your jogging cadence.

Psychologists tell us that if we act a certain way, our mental attitude will change accordingly. Many mornings I step out into my backyard and literally march around with my head up and my stomach in, saying out loud the words I have chosen to describe myself positively. Increased confidence is the certain payoff.

The keys to reprogramming your self-image are:

> **R** edescribe.
> **V** isualize.
> **R** epeat.

You can remember them with the memory jogger **RiVeR**—a river of positive influence flowing through your mind. That's using Memory Blueprint 1 (Initial Letters), with vowels added as "handles."

FIVE STEPS FOR MAINTAINING CONFIDENCE

If you are discouraged, depressed, or desperate, think of this memorable slogan: TRANSFORMATION NOT OBLITERATION. Then use five steps to help rebuild your confidence. To help you learn them quickly, here are the key terms for the five steps:

Five Steps for Maintaining Confidence

1. One thing
2. Act
3. Accentuate
4. Laser
5. Inner dialogue and affirmations

Using Memory Blueprint 9, construct the following sentence to cement the sequence of the key terms in your memory: **ONE THING ACTS** to **ACCENTUATE** my **LASER**like **INNER DIALOGUE** with **AFFIRMATIONS.**

One Thing at a Time. Trying to tackle everything all at once can get discouraging. Most of us find it easier to break large problems down into smaller, more doable tasks. So if you feel completely frustrated and blocked in your life, consider your total outlook and select just *one* viewpoint that you'd like to improve. Then repeat, over and over, the positive qualities based on your name to demonstrate to yourself that you *can* change that one part.

Maybe your immediate concern is that your current job feels like a dead end and you don't know what to do next. Don't let yourself get bogged down in feeling confused. Instead, use your mental energy to repeat your positive "name" qualities and visualize yourself in other situations where those qualities enabled you to take constructive action. Do this repeatedly, and soon you'll realize that you're evolving a plan, a list of workable solutions. But if you're also worrying at the same time about whether to invest in a limited partnership, you'll be much less effective at solving either problem.

Think of the exercise as restoring an old house—one room at a time. Gradually you'll be dwelling in restored, resourceful, and radiant awareness! To paraphrase a well-known couplet:

Success is not won at a single bound
But we fight life's battles round by round!

Acting As If. Behave like the kind of person you want to be, and before long you *will* be. It's not phony, although it may feel strange at first. It's not manipulative, although cynics might call it so. Of one thing I'm sure: it works!

Earle Nightingale, the dean of personal development, condensed his years of research on the causes of success into nine words: "We become what we think about all day long." Maxwell Maltz, the author of *Psycho-Cybernetics*, tells us to act as if we were already what we want to be.[1] Magic Johnson, famous basketball star, copied the best moves of other players; on the court he saw himself making all those wonderful moves, and this visualization influenced his success.

Cary Grant was an underprivileged poor boy in the slums of London. When he was about ten years old, he decided to *act like* some of the famous and distinguished people of England. He patterned himself on a combination of music hall stars Jack Buchanan, Noel Coward, and Rex Harrison and became like those men in real life.

Accentuating the Positive. It may sound like a cliché, but if it is, it's the most effective cliché in human history. When you're working on solving a personal dilemma, and all you can think of are the things that could go wrong, you're pretty well guar-

---

VISUALIZATION

Kirk Gibson limped to the plate with two out in the ninth in the first game of the 1988 World Series. The Los Angeles Dodger star was on the injury list but was sent in as a pinch hitter. He simply visualized what he wanted to have happen, relaxed, and hit the ball—for a game-winning home run. When Larry Mize won the 1987 Master's Golf Tournament with a 140-foot chip shot in sudden-death overtime, it was not a lucky shot. He was *aiming* for the hole, and he visualized the ball going in even before he hit it.

---

1. Maxwell Maltz, *Psycho-Cybernetics* (Old Tappan, N.J.: Pocket Books, 1983).

anteeing what will happen: failure. Pull out your list of positive qualities built around your name; doesn't that sound like a person who will make things go *right?*

If you are tempted to say, "I don't know what the future holds," substitute this phrase: "I don't know what great hours still await me." It makes life more exciting!

Laser Willpower. Use your willpower like a laser, with frequent short bursts of positive reinforcement. If you feel yourself wanting to procrastinate, shoot it with a laser blast of "Do it now." If you hear yourself thinking "I can't, . . ." zap that with "I can!" If some part of your mind protests "But I don't have the resources," your laser should immediately remind you, "Get them!"

Your Inner Dialogue. What is your inner dialogue doing to your identity? Is it positive or negative? Is it building you up or tearing you down? Is it poisoning you with a steady drip, drip, drip of discouragement and doubt, or is it feeding you with mental vitamins for vigor, poise, control, and promise? The thoughts you have about yourself are sometimes called self-talk, and some of them are poisonous. For example:

I'm beat.
I'm sick and tired.
I'm fed up.
I'm disgusted.
I'm at the end of my rope.
I'm running in place.
I'm beating my head against the wall.
I'm overworked.
I'm bogged down.
I've had it.
I can't stand it.
I've nowhere to go.
For two cents I'd tell 'em.
There's no future.
Leave me alone.

Get off my back.
Dump it.
It's the same old routine.
I hate it.
Take this job and. . . .

Once you become aware of what you're doing, you can use your memory to replace this destructive dialogue, as we'll see in the next step.

Affirmations and Antidotes. If your child swallowed some household poison, would you think, "Gee, I'm busy right now, but tomorrow when I'm down at the drugstore I'll see what they have for it"? Of course you wouldn't. You'd grab the phone, call the police, and yell, "My child's swallowed some poison! Help me, quick!" Yet every day we poison ourselves with negative self-talk and we delay applying the antidote.

Your first antidote consists of the positive words you selected to go with your name. They will flush negative poisons out of your mind fast. When you find yourself thinking, "I'm at the end of my rope," immediately say to yourself, "No I'm not; I am **R**esourceful, **I**ntelligent, **C**ompetent, and **K**nowledgeable [assuming your name is Rick], and I can find a solution to this." If you've repeated this list of positive qualities often, they will automatically spring into your conscious thought patterns, drowning out the negative self-talk.

Beyond this, you have to develop and memorize positive affirmations to serve as ready antidotes for specific thoughts that recur. If you've put on a little extra weight, and you feel depressed about it, the depression will diminish your effectiveness. So when you say to yourself, "I'm too heavy," instantly replace that with, "I have a strong and healthy body." If you're having difficulty making a major decision, don't make things harder on yourself by thinking, "I'm just no good at decisions." Instead, remind yourself, "I am a competent and able person, and I have made many good decisions in the past."

Reading and memorizing vigorous poetry is a good technique. It amplifies your memory power for positive words.

Henry Wadsworth Longfellow was suffering from a deep depression when he sat down one morning and wrote his vigorous "Psalm of Life." It became one of the most quoted poems in the English language. You may remember its closing stanza:

> *Let us now be up and doing,*
> *With a heart for any fate.*
> *Still achieving, still pursuing,*
> *Learn to labor and to wait.*

I cannot read aloud "Invictus," by William Henley—a poem very popular with inspirational speakers—without feeling courage rising within me. Try it yourself.

> *Out of the night that covers me,*
>   *Black as the Pit from pole to pole,*
> *I thank whatever gods may be*
>   *For my unconquerable soul.*
>
> *In the fell clutch of circumstance,*
>   *I have not winced nor cried aloud;*
> *Under the bludgeonings of chance*
>   *My head is bloody, but unbowed.*
>
>   *. . . .*
>
> *And yet the menace of the years*
>   *Finds and shall find me unafraid,*
>
> *It matters not how strait the gate*
>   *How charged with punishments the scroll,*
> *I am the master of my fate;*
>   *I am the captain of my soul.*

Songs are easily remembered and can exert a positive influence. Songs from college days, marches, great hymns, and popular songs are all sources of rhythmic reinforcement. Inspiring Scripture can be another great source of strength.

GETTING RID OF COMMON POISONS

Did you ever take a dose of one of these poisons?

If only I had a better education.
If only my boss appreciated me.

If only my family would give me a break.
If only he hadn't. . . .
If only she hadn't. . . .
If only my mother had. . . . If only my father had. . . .
If only I had a better territory.

The list is endless. Let me show you how I discovered a special antidote for this.

My friend Dave Yoho, author of the book *The EPOD Theory (How to Have a Great Year Every Year),*[2] is one of the most talented, dynamic public speakers and sales trainers in the country. He always concludes every presentation with Rudyard Kipling's poem "If." It puzzled me and many of his colleagues in the National Speakers Association why he continued to use "that old stuff." One day I wrote a humorous piece in which I suggested that he had been ordained to rescue all those who were always whining a long litany of "if only's." After listening to the great Yoho, I said, they thought only of the poem "If!"

It's fitting to quote the full poem here because it illustrates in memorable fashion both problems and antidotes. In it you will find sixteen goals, sixteen obstacles to their fulfillment, and sixteen mental solvents. Your memory blueprints can keep them at the tip of your mind.

> *If you can keep your head when all about you*
> *Are losing theirs and blaming it on you;*
> *If you can trust yourself when all men doubt you,*
> *But make allowance for their doubting too:*
> *If you can wait and not be tired by waiting,*
> *Or, being lied about, don't deal in lies,*
> *Or being hated don't give way to hating,*
> *And yet don't look too good, nor talk too wise;*
>
> *If you can dream—and not make dreams your master;*
> *If you can think—and not make thoughts your aim,*
> *If you can meet with Triumph and Disaster*
> *And treat those two imposters just the same;*
> *If you can bear to hear the truth you've spoken*
> *Twisted by knaves to make a trap for fools,*

2. Berkeley Press, 1989.

Or watch the things you gave your life to, broken,
  And stoop and build 'em up with worn-out tools;

If you can make one heap of all your winnings
  And risk it on one turn of pitch-and-toss,
And lose, and start again at your beginnings,
  And never breathe a word about your loss:
If you can force your heart and nerve and sinew
  To serve your turn long after they are gone,
And so hold on when there is nothing in you
  Except the Will which says to them: "Hold on!"

If you can talk with crowds and keep your virtue,
  Or walk with Kings—nor lose the common touch,
If neither foes nor loving friends can hurt you,
  If all men count with you, but none too much;
If you can fill the unforgiving minute
  With sixty seconds' worth of distance run,
Yours is the Earth and everything that's in it,
  And—which is more—you'll be a Man my son!

GOING FOR YOUR GOALS

With the power gained through positive thinking you will readily attain more dynamic, productive, and powerful goals. You'll keep your mind on target as never before. Your goals will be *positive* and **SMART**.

S   pecific
M   easurable
A   ttainable
R   ealistic
T   angible

Here is a stimulating and definite path to pursue in discovering definite goals:

1. Start with your business or career goals and ask yourself, "What goals do I have that can be described by a word beginning with *A*? With *B*? With *C*?" And so on.

2. Test each goal against the Positive and **SMART** Guide. Is it Positive? Specific? Measurable? Attainable? Realistic? Tangible?
3. Write down your words in alphabetical order.
4. Rearrange your goal words to form a memory blueprint.

For example, you may have these six goals:

1. Expand market in New Jersey.
2. Explore acquisition of smaller distributors.
3. Develop new product for snack line.
4. Plan further moves to decentralize.
5. Reorganize inventory controls.
6. Train—acquire a top training manager.

Using Memory Blueprint 1 (Initial Letters), you could rearrange those goals to spell the words **RED PET:**

> **R** *eorganize* inventory controls.
> **E** *xpand* market in New Jersey.
> **D** *evelop* new product for snack line.
>
> **P** *lan* further moves to decentralize.
> **E** *xplore* acquisition of smaller distributors.
> **T** *rain*—acquire a top training manager.

While the blueprint holds your goals firmly in your grasp, you can ponder them with the repetition that will rap them into your conscious awareness.

For help in identifying your goals, here are thought-starter goal words suggested by business executives and arranged alphabetically:

Acquire, amass, analyze, attack, attain, associate
Best, better, be active in organizations where professional and personal concerns are met
Conquer, care, carry out, challenge, continue
Develop
Employ, expand, explore
Find, finish, firm, freedom

Generate, gratify, gather, great, grow, growth

Help, have, hold, have a sense of opportunity

Increase leads, increase marketing, "I will do," impact, increase, influence

Join

Keep

Like, love

Money, means to help others, moderate

Networking (be more effective at)

Order, organize, overtake

Persevere, personal achievement, personal commitment, power

Question

Respect, rewarding

Satisfying, score, surpass, status

Tranquillity

GETTING TO KNOW THE REAL YOU

Broaden your vision when setting your goals; think of the several facets of "you"—the business you, the family you, the financial you, the romantic you, and the sports-loving you. John J. McCarthy, famous sales and management trainer, suggests that there are at least four aspects of each person:

1. The me I really am
2. The me I wish I were
3. The me I am trying to project to others
4. The me I think I am

When you are considering your "business you," bear in mind those four aspects. You might find that the goal of reorganizing inventory controls is "the me I am trying to project" but goes against "the me I really am," causing you to modify your goal and look for an individual to whom you can delegate the project completely. This analysis applies to every other area in your life. It will protect you from selecting, in the glow of enthusiasm or under pressure, a goal that you don't have the mind-set to carry out.

Your identity is the lively synthesis of the qualities and attributes that constitute your individuality. By holding in mind a clear sense of your own identity, you will strengthen your expression of your true self and ensure your progress.

You can test your various identities—business, personal, family—by using Memory Blueprint 1 and the memory jogger **IDENTITY**. Examine your:

> **I** nterests
> **D** esires
> **E** motions
> **N** ature
> **T** houghts
> **I** ndividuality
> **T** alk (self-talk, inner dialogue)

They all add up to

> **Y** our identity

After each word, list an activity or goal. For example:

Interests—marketing, finance, reading, golf
Desires—higher salary, new position, better office

As you become better acquainted with the real "you" stored by memory in the library of your mind, you will see new possibilities all around you.

CHOOSING A BETTER YOU

The motivational speaker Cavett Robert has on his wall a picture of a bum sitting by the road, watching a man in a Rolls Royce go by. The bum is saying, "There, but for me, go I."

Your choices will master you, whatever direction they take. Ask yourself, "Where are the choices I made today leading me? What has happened to me as a result of my choices?" In fact there is no area where you will achieve better results from the deliberate use of memory methods.

Some of the most difficult choices to implement are those involving long-standing habits. People with vital goals have learned to beware of bad habits, but some habits are difficult to break. Smoking, drinking, and overeating are three common habits from which many seek relief.

Salespeople know that the fear of loss is much stronger than the hope of gain. When it comes to bad habits, the penalties of continuing may be more persuasive than the benefits of quitting. So breaking habits is probably the only time it pays to remind yourself of negatives. For example, if you want to stop smoking, print the positive rewards for quitting smoking on one side of an index card and the penalties on the other, using Memory Blueprint 1 (Initial Letters). Then fasten the index card to your package of cigarettes.

Benefits	Penalties
C leanliness	**C** ancer
I ndependence	**I** nducing
G reat feeling	**G** uaranteed
A ctivity	**A** ctivating
R esourcefulness	**R** espiratory
E nergy	**E** mphysema
T errific	**T** errible
T riumphant	**T** orturous
E xcitement	**E** xit

Don't try to stop smoking! Whenever you reach for a cigarette, read over both sides of your card. Your subconscious will start to *relieve* you of the habit. It won't take too many readings to build the benefits and penalties into your inner guidance system, which will keep you on your chosen course.

The two-martini lunch has become a legend in business circles. If alcohol presents a problem you would like to control, try the following memory joggers **MARTINI** and **ALCOHOL**:

M	asks	**A**	lways
A	bility	**L**	essens
R	educes	**C**	ontrol
T	alent	**O**	ften
I	mpedes	**H**	ampers
N	ew	**O**	rganized
I	nitiatives	**L**	ife

The same type of memory jogger applies to other forms of substance abuse. Using the generic word **DRUGS,** think:

D	irectly
R	educes
U	sefulness
G	uarantees
S	lippage

Is weight a problem? Over the years I have probably "mislaid" a couple of hundred pounds by taking off twenty or twenty-five at a time through dieting and then putting them back by self-indulgence. Finally I realized I had to make choices, and I have been able to maintain a satisfactory weight level for years.

For your freedom path, an "amble down the alphabet" can help you identify the dietary foes and saboteurs and create memory joggers to help you eliminate them. First step: Identify the foes. I'll do the first six letters of the alphabet to get you started:

A	lcohol
B	read, butter
C	ake, cookies
D	oughnuts, desserts
E	clairs
F	udge

Now pick your personal enemies. Let's say you decide that **A**lcohol, **C**ake, **E**clairs, and **F**udge are four particular enemies. Rearrange their initials to make a memory jogger: **CAFE.**

Now line up friendly alternatives to your worst enemies. For continuity of thought, make them rhyme with or start with the same letters as the enemy word. With this list of friends, you'll always have an "instead" ready:

Instead of **ALCOHOL**, I'll drink **APPLE JUICE**.

Instead of **BREAD** and **BUTTER**, I'll nibble **BROCCOLI**.

Instead of **CAKE** and **COOKIES**, I'll chew a **CARROT**.

Instead of **DOUGHNUTS and DESSERTS**, I'll take **DRIED** fruits.

Instead of **ECLAIRS**, I'll take **PEARS**.

Instead of **FUDGE**, I'll have some **FRUIT**.

Keep your worst enemies in your mental sights by creating memory joggers.

B	roadens	**C**	reates
R	ear	**A**	pathy
E	xtends	**K**	ills
A	bdomen	**E**	xpectation
D	efeats diet		
		D	efeats
B	ulges	**E**	easily
U	nnecessary	**S**	educes
T	reacherous	**S**	elf
T	empter	**E**	xactly
E	xcessive	**R**	uins
R	ear	**T**	riumph

When you're tempted to snack on bread to quell your nervousness, especially when dining out where you start on rolls and butter, review your negative words based on **BREAD**. Your subconscious will get the message and become your ally if you *feed it* the right messages.

I used to be tempted to grab a candy bar when I was on the run at airports; my excuse was that I needed quick energy. Then one night I was on a radio interview show with a diet specialist who talked about the dangers of sugar to the human body. He started by saying that it increases the **C**holesterol, **U**ric acid, and **T**ryglycerides in the blood. The initial letters spelled **CUT**, and I decided right then to **CUT** it out. Whenever I was tempted to buy my favorite candy bar, I stood before the candy counter and mentally went through what **CUT** stood for. It worked!

You can also create an alphabet based on desirable objectives, such as:

> **A** ctive
> **B** eautiful
> **C** omplete
> **D** esirable
> **E** nergetic

Make your own individual complete alphabet. After you have worked through it for a week, the regular repetition will implant the rewards and warnings in your permanent awareness, where they will automatically protect you.

To summarize:

> **C** reate
> **H** elpful
> **O** ptimistic
> **I** ntentions
> **C** oncentrate
> **E** nthusiastically

4

Remembering
Names and Faces

Has anyone ever said to you, "I remember your name but I can't remember your face"? Probably not. More likely you've heard, "I can remember faces but not names."

How should we go about remembering faces and the names that go with them? First, it's essential to consider the face a picture, since most of us remember pictures we've already seen. If I stood before you now, you'd probably say instantly that you'd never seen me before. Think of that! What a marvelous memory you have for pictures. Your mental computer scanned the thousands of pictures stored in your mind and instantly said, "This one doesn't match."

All you have to do to remember names is to put them into the most powerful form: *pictures.* You wouldn't dream of talking to a computer in anything but computer language. So let's talk to your memory bank in the language it accepts and processes most easily.

EASY AS 1 - 2 - 3

Remembering names and faces is a three-step procedure:

1. Observe the face.
2. Observe the name.
3. Associate the name with the face.

Step 1: Observe the Face. For a week play a game to sharpen your ability to notice differences in individual appearances. Increasing your power of observation will automatically increase your power of association. Each day study a different aspect of faces.

Monday. Look at mouths. When you start becoming aware of details, you will quickly see that there are more shapes and sizes of mouths than you realized. Develop your own descriptive words or thoughts for each. Consider what attitude the lips express.

Tuesday. Observe noses. As you commute to work, notice profiles and other differences.

Wednesday. Look at ears. The ear was considered a distinctive feature long before fingerprints came into use. Notice the many variations of shape, position, and other individual features.

Thursday. Observe hair. Notice how varieties of style, color, and texture create individual effects.

Friday. Observe people's eyes. Notice how deeply set, how wide apart they are, the color and shape of the lashes.

Saturday. Look at head shapes. See a prominent forehead, a wide chin, broad cheekbones; notice various curves and bumps.

You'll be amazed and amused by how accomplished you have become in the skill of observation. By week's end a variety of significant variations in your pictures of faces will flood your consciousness. You can perfect this procedure by analyzing faces of television newscasters and verbally characterizing features.

Observing body language also will help sharpen your ability to see differences and add meaning to the individuals you study.

Let's practice by visualizing faces of people you already know. Make a list of seven. Think about the first person on your list. What characteristics of that face first came to mind? It doesn't have to be favorable or even something you'd ever mention, just what *you* first thought about when describing that person *to yourself.* For instance, you might think he has a big nose. Never mind what anyone else thinks. If you think it's big, it is. Now do the same for the other six. When you think of each person, what one facial characteristic springs to mind? Review all seven faces you selected and mentally recall your first reaction. If you noticed the nose, enlarge it as a cartoonist would. It it's a scar, make it deeper. If the person has white hair, make it longer or shorter. Make keen blue eyes even bluer.

Association plays a strong role here. As you practice observing people during the week, stick with the first feature that strikes you. I'm not suggesting that the first person you selected *has* a big nose, but whatever the feature is that strikes you, exaggerate it. Your first reaction is the most important. Don't try to describe that person fully to yourself.

Perhaps that feature reminds you of someone you know and you say to yourself, "He looks like the CEO." Perhaps it's an impression of an occupation—for example, "He looks like a banker; she looks like a model."

Step 2: Observe the Name. By "observe the name," I mean: Really *see* it; make a picture of it. Remember that our brains generally remember pictures best, so create some kind of visual image that captures whatever that name means to you.

To understand how this step works, let's practice with some fairly easy Anglo-Saxon surnames derived from trades: Carpenter, for example. What would your picture be for Carpenter? Mine happens to be my second-grade teacher, but you might visualize a woodworking tool. What picture do you see for someone named Barber? Pretty easy, right?

Now try these. What picture comes to mind when you think:

Berry?
Shoemaker?
Mason?
Gardner?
Mellon?
Gray?
Lyon?

You've already visualized features of these seven people you know. Now invent a new name for each from the above list.

Step 3: Associate the Name With the Face. My name, Hersey, is easy to picture. Most people think of a Hershey bar. Since I have white hair, I suggest they picture me rubbing my white hair with a chocolate Hershey bar to make it brown. I suggest further they talk to themselves about this unusual practice, using my name at least three times. Now it *may* seem to go against your image of yourself as a sensible, intelligent person, but do try it and *see* the surprising results. It is OK to use the illogical for a logical purpose.

Now make a pictorial association between the facial feature you noted in step 1 and the picture you created for the name in step 2.

FACE PICTURE + NAME PICTURE = THE PERSON YOU WANT TO REMEMBER

Practice using your natural ability for pictorial associations by linking the features of the seven individuals whom you already know with the seven easily visualized names given in step 2. Forget for a moment their real names. This is for visual practice.

The first name is Berry. Try to associate your picture for berry with the feature you selected and exaggerated for the first person on your list. Yes, even if it's your CEO, you can picture squashing berries onto or into the features you selected. Stop now and really try this.

Let's do one more. Give the second person on your list the name Shoemaker, and associate your picture for shoemaker with the feature you selected. It is sometimes helpful to imagine how a TV commercial would enforce the association.

Talk to yourself about that special feature, repeating the name while you are looking at the person. Make vivid, exaggerated, and memorable statements, using the name at least three times.

Up to this point you have been associating new pictorial names with people you already know. Now practice this winning skill with faces and names both of which are new to you. You have several readily available sources: TV news, TV entertainment, newspapers, and magazines.

By using your VCR to tape some broadcasts, you can stop the action; that way you gain time to lock the name to the face or general appearance.

One word of caution: Whatever visual images you use, you must get the name right or your brain will give up. The human mind resists remembering anything that is incomplete or indefinite.

OTHER TECHNIQUES

I've stressed the technique of picturing names, but there are other methods of remembering names and faces. One is to make an association based on *appearance*. For instance, recently at a concert I noticed the kettle drummer and immediately thought, "He looks like Henry Kissinger." If I saw him again I'd think, "This is the kettle drummer who looks like Henry Kissinger." And if I had a chance to learn his name on that occasion, I'd make an association based on the Kissinger resemblance. If his name turned out to be, say, Templeton, I'd remember Kissinger as Secretary of State visiting all the temples in the Middle East.

I could also make an association based on *meaning*—that is, on the meaning this particular individual has for me. I would visualize Mr. Templeton standing in front of a grand temple, solemnly beating his kettle drum. In this particular case, of course, I could also combine the two images.

Think over some of the people whose names you have forgotten and notice what you do remember about them. You will discover it's either their appearance or the meaning they had for you. If you encounter the name again, tie it to either appearance or meaning and lock it into your permanent memory. Thinking of three or four descriptive statements, using either meaning or appearance and including the name with each, is a quiet, private, and magical way to remember names. Do this for about twenty seconds with each name.

Another way to remember a name is to find a similar-sounding word. For example, I once met a woman named Benke. She said people had trouble remembering her name, so I suggested she tell them to think of "banking on Benke." Another example: The name Albanese sounds like "Albany" to me.

A good way to remember long names is to break them into syllables and then make whatever association comes to mind. A name that stuck in my mind for years was Boodakian, one of about seventy Armenian names I learned one evening. I pictured Mr. Boodakian scaring someone by saying "Boo!" in the dark. Twelve years later I recognized the name on a transcontinental flight and discovered I was speaking to his son.

One of the first long names I learned to remember was Papayanokos. My father suggested remembering it as PAPA YOU KNOW OF COURSE. This provided a pattern of words with meaning to use as a bridge to help in remembering the real name.

Here are a few names and the meanings I see in the syllables. Your meanings may well be different.

Ambushadi—AMBUSH HAD I

Chuprinski—CHEW PRINCE SKI

Kirkor—KIRK OR

Bonez—BONES

Buccola—A BUCK FOR A COLA

Adlam—ADD LAMB

Recktenwold—WRECK TEN WORLDS

Raitzin—RATES SIN

Ahmud—AH MUD

You can also use rhymes to add meaning; for instance, "Mr. Dewire's hat's on fire." The word "fire" has special meaning, and when you think of it, the rhyming association will bring back the name. This method is often used at demonstration sales parties. Each guest gives a first name and rhymes it with a meaningful word: "I'm Mary and I'm scary." "I'm Ruth and that's the truth."

Finally, some names lend themselves to backward spelling. I met a lawyer named Riaf. He said, "It's 'fair' spelled backward, and you always get a fair deal from Riaf the lawyer." Oprah Winfrey uses her name spelled backward for her production company, Harpo Productions.

So, all together I've described seven ways to remember names. Pick what you think will work for you.

1. Names as pictures
2. Names and appearance
3. Names and meaning
4. Name sounds
5. Names in syllables
6. Rhyming names
7. Names spelled backward

TO LEARN NAMES, TRY LISTENING

Another way to remember names, faces, and information about people is to apply the six rules of personal empowerment. If you recall the discussion in Chapter 2, the rules are:

L *isten*. People respect and reward good listeners.
I *nterest*. Show an interest.
S *mile*.
T *alk*. Encourage them to talk.

I *important*. Make them feel important.
N *ame*. Use the name. It's a tribute to their identity.

You can remember it with the memory jogger **LIST IN.**

The deliberate use of these six rules is a new breakthrough in remembering things about people. If you consciously practice these rules in the first sixty seconds you meet someone, you will greatly increase your acceptance and influence.

You must *listen* and get the name right; that's rule 1. When I meet new people I usually have the name spelled or check the spelling. Yes, even for Smith. I ask, "Is that just a plain old-fashioned S-m-i-t-h?" Sometimes it isn't! But asking the question does indicate that you are paying attention—**LIST**ening and showing an **IN**terest.

Remember how you felt when someone took the time to really remember your name? Now you'll see how this can make you an instant winner when you make that special effort to get the name right. No matter how long it takes, the other person will love every second of it!

All individuals have some significance for us, some interest or meaning. In most cases you wouldn't be meeting them if there was no interest. It may be the man from IBM, the new receptionist, the woman who is interested in developing markets in Spain, or the artist from your advertising agency. They all have some meaning for you. Depending on your interest, you will remember each person differently. So take advantage of rule 2 to help remember a person's name by connecting the interest with the name.

We all seem to remember *things* about people more easily than
their names. You can ask questions to bring out meaning when
you meet people for the first time. Ask intelligent or even personal questions, but don't waste the opportunity by discussing
trivial matters.

One of my favorite questions for openers is, "Do you come
from around here?" You'll be surprised how many people are
from somewhere else and like to talk about it. While they are
answering, you can build more and better associations with their
name. Other common questions are "What do you do?" or
"What's your profession?"

You can even turn trivial topics into something memorable. If
someone mentions the weather, ask what he thinks of today's
weather. If it's very cold, ask, "What's the coldest weather you
ever experienced?" As your new acquaintance talks, you will have
plenty of time to make associations with his name.

Recently I was introduced to a woman and casually remarked,
"Isn't this a great day?"

"Yes," she answered. Not much to go on.

"If you could control the weather," I asked, "what would you
order?"

Much to my surprise, she said, "I really like cold, damp, gray
days." That sparked a conversation of several minutes, which
gave me ample time to make an association between her name
and her weather comments, and also with her appearance.

Beyond these openers, the field is yours. Ask people for their
opinion on some aspect of current events or something applica-
ble to their business. Get them talking and keep them talking;
you keep listening and associating the name, and it will stick.
Keep them talking by saying, "That's very interesting; can you
tell me more about it?" or "Could you expand on that point?"

Try questioning. You'll like it and you'll develop a reputation
as an interesting conversationalist even if you say only a few
words. It takes about twenty seconds for a name to "set" in your
memory bank. You gain those twenty seconds by controlling the
conversation and using the time in which the other person is
talking to carry on your own inner dialogue, locking the name
to the face, appearance, or meaning.

When you run into a difficult name, *never* say, "That's an odd
name." Instead, say, "That's an interesting name" or "That's an

---

GLUE

If you're gluing two boards together for a table top and the directions say, "Let set for ten hours," you don't try to put them to use in less time. They'd fall apart. But if you let them set, they'll be permanently bonded together and appear as one board. There's a certain setting time for information in your mind. With names it's about twenty seconds. With more extensive information it may take two or three days of intermittent repetition. Discover the time frame that works best for you and stick with it.

---

unusual name; what's its origin?" One morning very early at a trade show I met a man who was busily setting up an exhibit. His name tag read SIKORSKY, and when I asked, "Like the man who invented the helicopter?" he took five minutes out of his busy time to give me—a stranger he'd probably never see again—the family history and the variations in spelling. He proved that people love it when you talk about their names!

So . . . you have been listening, showing an interest, and smiling (don't forget the immense power of a genuine smile) while you've been encouraging the person to talk about himself. You have made him feel important, and you will be ready and confident to use his name. You have brought the six rules of personal empowerment to work for you, probably in fewer than sixty seconds.

REMEMBERING ONE NAME OUT OF MANY

How valuable are names to you? If someone handed you a bottle of wine worth $25,000, you'd certainly take extra care not to drop it. A person's name is worth more than the wine. *Don't drop it!*

You have to carefully and consciously store names with faces every single time, just as a file clerk has to deliberately file each piece of correspondence. A file clerk picks up speed with practice, and so will you.

When you are meeting groups of people, use this magic rule: After you've met three people, look back at them and check your memory for their names. Then continue on and look back at three

more. This three-at-a-time review is vital; it guarantees that you
will catch yourself on any omissions before you try to absorb too
much.

When you are attending a conference where name badges or
names on tent cards on the tables are used, start working with
two or three names at a time. Keep in mind the following:

- Notice the same people during breaks. Many look quite different when they are standing rather than sitting.
- Keep reinforcing your memory. Work systematically. *Intend*
  to remember names. Don't depend on the name badges or
  cards.
- Keep a list of the names of those you have met and review it.

At less formal occasions, such as cocktail parties and dinners
when you have time to circulate and chat individually, follow
these three easy steps:

1. Visit with an *intention* to remember names.
2. After you've met two or three people, look back at them
   and repeat their names to yourself. Then move on.
3. Keep rechecking the first three names, then the first six.
   Then every time you add three more, review the previous six.

If drinks are being served, nurse the first until you've met
everyone. Alcohol increases your self-confidence, but it weakens
your memory.

I can hear you saying, "But frequently I'm introduced so rapidly that I don't have time to get any names." Welcome to the
club. Sometimes I can't keep hosts from pushing others at me
too fast. So after a break I recirculate deliberately and at my own
pace. I approach someone and say, "I'm sorry, but we were introduced so rapidly that I didn't get your name clearly; would
you please tell it to me again?" They love the attention. Sometimes I've even gone back a second time and said, "You know,
I'm in real trouble tonight. I've just lost your name again."

You can further reinforce your memory for new acquaintances
if you drop them a note. "I was glad to have met you and I'm

particularly interested in the thought you expressed about. . . . I'd appreciate it greatly if you could expand on that or direct me to some further information." This adds meaning about the individual and impact to your memory.

REMEMBERING FIRST NAMES

So far we've dealt mostly with last names because first names come last when picking up names. You can call someone by his last name even in social or informal situations, and there's nothing wrong with using such shortcuts to help yourself. However, when you do want to remember first names, a good technique is to use the last name as a "hook" to hang the first on, like a picture.

For instance, you may have pictured my name Hersey as a Hershey bar. My first name is Bill. If you ever saw a dollar bill with the Hershey logo printed in the middle, you'd probably never forget it. I frequently tie in pictures of first names that have meaning for me. For instance, the name Charles always conjures up the face of my brother Charles, and I use my brother-in-law Robert as a standard picture for Robert.

GIVING YOURSELF THE WINNING EDGE

You will have the winning edge, the influential edge, if you take just a few minutes to memorize something about the people attending a meeting before you get there. This strategy launched my career in memory. When I was selling mutual funds I wanted to give an educational talk (not a sales presentation) about mutual funds to service clubs as a means of widening my acquaintance in the community. I secured the roster of members in advance and memorized each person's name and business connection.

As I circulated among the tables I'd say, "Tell me just your last name, please." If the person replied "Miller," I'd say, "Oh, yes, you're George Miller, the civil engineer." This gave me instant and favorable influence.

Another example occurred some years ago. I had an idea that

I thought might be of interest to either *Life* or *Time* Magazine. My friend Jim Mosely said, "You ought to talk to Nick Samstag of *Time* Magazine, who wrote *Persuasion for Profit.*" He gave me a copy of the book, and I read it and underlined the key points. Later, when I was introduced to the author, I said, "Mr. Samstag, I've been reading your book. I was particularly interested in what you said about persuasion. Could you elaborate on that?" He did, and Time-Life hired me soon after for an important presentation.

This strategy can work for you! Suppose you are meeting with a group; perhaps it's a sales situation. You have prepared in advance and know that Ernest Martin has experience in building power plants and that Joseph Warren has explored for oil. When you meet them, you can acknowledge their achievements in conversation. You can bet they will remember you, and they'll have a favorable estimate of your abilities.

You can use Memory Blueprint 7 (The Chain) to memorize names and information about people in advance. Let's see how you can remember four names and some information on each.

Think of someone you know named Fred. Have you pictured him? Pretend his last name is Painter. Fred Painter is a broker. Put together in your own mind a picture linking (chaining) Fred with Painter with "broker." I see Fred painting stock prices in big red letters; I'm sure you can think of other imaginative ways of linking those three points into one memorable mental mural. Pause now while you paint the picture on the murals of your mind. Now, what is Painter's first name? His business? Simple, wasn't it?

Let's try another. The first name is Jacqueline. Her last name is Gray and she's a computer consultant. Link your picture for Jacqueline to your picture for Gray to your picture for computer consultant to form a chain. Do it now. Exaggeration will help in this exercise.

What is Gray's first name? Business? Painter's first name? Business?

Let's try another. The first name is Arthur and the last is Long. Arthur Long is a sales manager. Link your picture for these three elements into an unforgettable mental mural. What is Long's first name? Business? Gray's first name? Business? Painter's first name? Business?

Let's do one more, because I want you to realize you can process four names in just about four minutes. The first name is Ted and the last name is Cohen and he is a real estate developer. Paint that picture before continuing.

What is Cohen's first name? Business? Who is the sales manager? The computer consultant? The broker?

Here are ten more names. Practice systematically with your pictures for the first name, last name, and business, all linked together in one unforgettable mental mural or chain.

David Herald, banker
Daniel Fuller, sports writer
Angela Swanson, editor
Roberta White, accountant
Robert Swab, insurance
John Cousins, Coca-Cola
Arthur Read, engineer
William Rose, builder
Shelly Patel, The Sand Bar
Hazel Hiram, real estate

Keep a separate list of just last names, and glance over it each time you add a new name. It will help guarantee that you have pictured the three elements vividly.

Mentally storing names and information in advance is one of the most influential skills you can develop. You can easily get ready to meet ten people with ten minutes of preparation time. That's how to guarantee the winning edge when you walk into a meeting, interview, or conference.

TWO SPECIAL APPLICATIONS

Your ability to memorize information about people in advance gives you a golden opportunity in two situations that most people find very stressful: being interviewed for a job, and being transferred to another business location. In the case of a transfer, knowing the key names will aid greatly in fitting yourself into a new environment. Before your first day of work, learn the names and job titles of those you will be working with. If you encounter difficult or unusual names, you can probably find out in advance exactly how to pronounce them by calling the company switchboard. Nothing pleases a person more than to have his unusual surname pronounced correctly. Let's say Bob Gianelli is the controller—an important person to know. You'll gain a distinct advantage because you recognize his name and know how to pronounce it and because you know his title.

During a job interview you will find that knowing the names of people in advance will make you more impressive. Learn as much as you can about those with whom you will be dealing and the names of other key personnel in the organization. No need to show off, but you will certainly receive credit for having done your homework.

BE YOUR OWN CHEERLEADER EVERY DAY

With the names you already know, you can automatically increase your ability to remember other names. It will get you off to a good start every day. Instead of just saying, "Good morning," say "Good morning, Angela," or "Good morning, Fred." When you use people's names, they will light up in a smile. Pretty soon you'll be smiling too. Psychologists tell us that we feel happy *because* we are smiling, not smiling because we feel happy. This is why I call it being your own cheerleader. The good reactions you receive when you use people's names will automatically motivate you to remember other names better.

You can apply the memory blueprints in this book to create an outstanding ability to remember the most important asset of any business—people. Memory, the golden goddess, leads the way to lifetime influence.

5

Listening Better—And Remembering More

His speech was slow,
His words were plain
And never meant to glisten.
But he was a joy wher'ere he went,
You should have heard him listen!

— FRED HERRMAN, sales trainer

Albert L. Nickerson, who became president of Mobil Oil before he was age 40, was an outstanding and impressive listener. Long before he became president, he frequently conducted conferences with those in the company who were much older than he. How did he handle those situations? He listened. When everyone had made his contribution to the discussion, he systematically and completely reviewed what each person had said, directed attention to key points, and only then brought his own viewpoint into the discussion. With this pattern of thorough listening, he acknowledged the experience and intelligence of everyone present and also demonstrated his own ability.

Nickerson's impressive ability to recap everything that was said and focus on the key points is a testimony to one fundamental rule: Memory is basic to good listening. If you don't remember what has been said, you haven't really listened.

In our mouth-to-ear information society, much more information is communicated in informal conversations than in formal presentations. Thus, it is essential in business that we understand and retain accurately what another person is telling us. Sometimes the problem is not so much forgetting as "not getting"!

Noted management expert John J. McCarthy says in his dynamic book *Why Managers Fail*, "Many managers share a common human weakness; i.e., they are poor listeners! In spite of this, in an effort to halt the mounting avalanche of paper work with which most organizations are afflicted, management in many enterprises is imploring employees to resist the impulse to send memos, and to use the phone instead."[1]

ARE YOU A GOOD LISTENER?

Few people like to admit that they don't listen. The following exercises will let you evaluate how well you retain the spoken word. Check yourself.

Exercise 1. Listen to a television or radio newscast for five minutes. Record it or have someone take notes. At the end of five minutes, see how many topics you can jot down. Then compare your performance with the actual broadcast.

Exercise 2. Have someone read the following instructions to you slowly and carefully. See if you can pick up the necessary details the first time without asking for repeats.

> Take your car, this afternoon, and go to Dulles Airport. You are to meet Delta's Flight 345, which arrives at 2:30 P.M. You are to meet Mr. Albert and drive him to Baltimore to the Federal Building. Take him to room 1101 and introduce him to Mr. Gustafson. When you have accomplished this, call me, and tomorrow morning bring in your expense vouchers and we'll pay them.

How well did you listen? I have tried this test on thousands and found that most people ask for repeats after the first sentence. Those with special training are very good at remembering details of this type. For instance, a group of high-ranking army officers and CIA personnel excelled, but were no better than average at remembering information on other types of listening tests.

WHY IS LISTENING SO HARD?

Researchers on the subject of listening emphasize one main problem: People remember only about half of what they've just

1. New York: Mc-Graw Hill.

heard. Researchers have also identified eight common obstacles to good listening:

1. Prejudging the subject or the speaker
2. Pretending attention while the mind is somewhere else
3. Not thinking objectively about the matter
4. Permitting distractions to interfere
5. Avoiding difficult material
6. Being overstimulated by the speaker's remarks to the point of interrupting and failing to hear her out
7. Turning off a poor speaker because of his dress, accent, speech, or poor organization
8. Thinking faster than the speaker

Few of us want to admit that any of these obstacles apply to us, but we can think of someone else—our boss or our spouse, maybe—who has these problems. But in fact, most of us are not the calm, judicious, receptive, and objective listeners we think we are.

The principal barrier to effective listening is the difference in speed between thinking and talking. For example: What did you have for breakfast? As soon as you read that question your mind went through a process that would have taken you several seconds to express. You can *think* "Orange juice, toast, eggs, and coffee" in a fraction of a second. But it would take you four or five times as long to actually speak those words.

We think at about 1,200 words per minute, but the maximum speed at which we talk is not much over 200 words per minute. On average, a person speaks at only 100 to 150 words per minute. So you can see that the mind has a great deal of spare time in which to wander off!

What's the solution? How can you keep your mind from wandering? Take a clue from baseball players. If you watch the outfielders in a professional game, you'll notice they change positions with every batter and sometimes with every pitch. They are recalling the batter's record and receiving signals from the coaches as to where the batter is most likely to hit a particular pitch. The outfielders must constantly stay in the same part of the ball park with the batter's potential in order to be in a position to catch the ball. At the end of the game, the announcer says, "Well, the

Sox hit three long balls today, but every one of them was right at somebody." And that's no accident. To put it another way: The fielders know how to be at the probable termination point of each hit.

When you're listening, you have to "stay in the ball park" with a speaker by paying enough attention to be able to respond intelligently to what is being said.

INCREASING YOUR LISTENING POWER

You can stay with the train of thought by following these four steps and using your favorite memory blueprint.

Step 1: Practice Listening. Listen to a five-minute newscast. *Really* listen, and reinforce what you hear by using your favorite memory blueprint to remember it.

For example, here are ten topics from a five-minute newscast, including commercials:

1. President
2. Budget
3. Deficit
4. Back pain
5. Murder
6. Weather
7. Traffic
8. Antacid
9. Stock market
10. Tornado

Maybe you can remember the topics best with Memory Blueprint 3 (Rhyming Words). As a reminder, the rhyming words for the numbers one through ten are: "gun," "shoe," "tree," "door," "dive," "sticks," "heaven," "gate," "wine," and "hen." For the first item, you might picture the President together with a gun.

Or maybe you'd find it easier to remember a string of items by making a chain (Memory Blueprint 7): The PRESIDENT is signing his name to a new BUDGET package that is designed to reduce the DEFICIT.

Whatever works best for you, visualization practice is vital here. Your ability to create pictures will automatically improve your listening skills. It will stimulate your ability to "see" what you are hearing even in casual communication and produce a habit of concentration in all listening situations.

Step 2: Let the Speaker Finish! Hear the speaker out. Listen intently. You may be tempted to let your mind race ahead (remember the difference in hearing speed and speaking speed), especially if it's a topic you are familiar with. But resist that temptation. For one thing, even though you think you know what she's going to say, you could be wrong; if you let your mind wander you could miss a significant shift. Then there is the simple matter of courtesy. And finally, even if you are mentally ahead, stay with the speaker and use the points she's making as on-the-spot practice for a memory blueprint you want to strengthen.

Don't let yourself be drawn into evaluations until you are certain you have a complete understanding. *You* must manage the conversation.

Step 3: Replay Before You Reply. Before you comment on what you've been listening to, summarize the key points the other person made. You'll accomplish two things with this recap: You

---

THE FAST THINKER

He was an able and brilliant production manager, but he was frequently in hot water with the vice-president to whom he reported.

I spent a day with him and discovered that the heart of the problem was that he was a much faster thinker than the vice-president. He tended to jump in with his viewpoints before the vice-president had finished. When he interrupted at important meetings, such as budget sessions with top management, the net effect was belittling to the vice-president.

This manager was smart, no doubt about it. He realized the need and learned how to solve the problem. I showed him how to use memory blueprints to keep his mind on the track and to store every point the vice-president made. He disciplined himself to replay what the vice-president had said before replying. He tells me it worked like a charm.

will thoroughly set the ideas in your mind, and you'll make a very powerful impression.

Let's say someone is discussing a new marketing program with you. You can demonstrate your ability to grasp concepts completely by using Memory Blueprint 3 (Rhyming Words). At an appropriate pause you say, "Al, that's very interesting. As I understand it there are eight aspects of the program. They are. . . ." and then play them back before making any further comment. You will make a powerful impression.

Step 4: Tactfully Ask for a Repeat. In many listening situations you'll find that the speaker is not well organized, doesn't speak clearly, and beats around the bush. In spite of your best efforts, certain distractions, emotions, stress, or other factors may cause you to miss some points in an important business conversation. In that case, you must encourage the other person to repeat what was said, and you must find a way to do it without embarrassing either one of you. You can apply the following face-saving phrases as first aid. Use the memory jogger **THE CREW** to show you what to do and help you take command.

"**T** ell me more." Or, "What do you **T**hink?"
"**H** ow did this happen?"
"**E** xpand." "Could you *expand* on that?"

"**C** onsider." "What do you *consider* to be. . . ?"
"**R** ecap or **R**eview." "Could you *recap* (or *review*) those points?"
"**E** xplain." "Could you *explain* that a little further?"
"**W** hy?" Or "What?"

Here's how to apply this first aid. When you miss something in a conversation, start your response with the two magic words "That's interesting!" Then take a deep breath to show you are considering what was said and say, "Tell me more."

The word *expand* is extremely valuable here. You can use it in a specific way. For instance, suppose there are six points and you are missing the fourth but don't want to ask about it specifically. Instead say, "If I understand you correctly you made six points. Could you expand on the third one about the new budget policy?" The chances are the other person will pick up on the third and cover the fourth as well.

TECHNIQUES FOR SPECIAL SITUATIONS

Listening at Conferences. If you'd like to be as impressive as A. L. Nickerson, the young president of Mobil, there is a way to practice alone. Educational television offers many discussion programs that simulate a conference situation. They are reasonably paced and provide an excellent opportunity to practice picking up points from several speakers. My favorite for this is *Washington Week in Review*, where the moderator outlines topics for discussion and asks each of the panelists to discuss problems in their field of expertise.

To practice, record the program and then review it with your VCR so you can control the speed. Listen to one panelist, stop the tape, and then pretend to talk to that person about what was said. If you missed something, imagine yourself using one of **THE CREW** phrases to encourage repetition. For instance, recently a panelist was discussing the contributions made by various retiring members of Congress. If you had forgotten what she had said about a certain senator, you could imagine yourself saying, "You made several interesting observations about the senator. Could you recap them for me, please?"

Play a game of imaginary response and conversation with each panelist. Those conference-listening techniques will soon become habitual.

Rush-Order Listening. The television program *Wall Street Week* provides many opportunities for rush-order listening. For instance, what do you do when a guest recommends ten stocks in about ten seconds? This is a situation where there is no time to take notes or even start plunking names down on your house blueprint. What can you do?

Remember the knight in shining armor serving up Wheaties in Chapter 2? That was the first two links in a chain (Memory Blueprint 7). You could use that or Memory Blueprint 8 (The Stack) to visualize pictures that represent to you the names of the stocks. First repeat the names as they are given. Then create your chain (or stack), and review them again instantly before writing them down. You can practice in high-speed situations with your VCR.

Verbatim Listening. Business listening seldom requires the ability to repeat another's words exactly. But sometimes it *is* necessary—for example, in a confidential situation where no notes are taken. But it takes practice. We humans have a natural tendency to mentally rephrase what another person has said in the words we would have used to express the same idea. I have played a recording of a twenty-two-word statement at seminars and asked the participants to write down exactly what was said. There is seldom anyone who can write down those twenty-two words accurately. To practice verbatim listening, tape record a very short statement from a news program. See if you can repeat word for word exactly what was said. Then practice with longer and longer excerpts.

Listening Under Stress. When the speaker is angry, you may have difficulty remembering accurately what has been said. Defusing a situation before you reply is a valuable listening strategy and an important aid to your ability to remember under stress.

In addition to the first-aid phrases summarized by **THE CREW,** there are some special phrases you can use to help soothe emotions that are running high. Getting the speaker to repeat or explain further will reduce the emotional content before you give your viewpoint. These phrases require you to make concessions, but they work. Try these three:

1. "I can see you feel very strongly about that. Tell me more."
2. "I see you feel very strongly about that and I'm sure you have some excellent reasons for feeling as you do. Tell me more."
3. "If I were in your shoes I'd probably feel exactly as you do. Tell me more."

By using these phrases you not only gain time to clarify your response, but you'll be able to remember the key points of the conversation, which could have been obscured by the initial blast of strong emotion.

6

Making Every Minute Count

If you can fill the unforgiving minute
With sixty seconds' worth of distance run,
Yours is the Earth and everything that's in it."

—RUDYARD KIPLING

One hour alone is in thine hands
The now on which the shadow stands!

—HENRY VAN DYKE,
Speaking of the Sundial

We all live and act on the narrow edge of now, and, as with the sundial, there is always the shadow of necessity or distraction on the present hour. We are all concerned about time management, but actually we don't manage time—we manage personal activity and performance.

Here, in just ten words, is the bedrock of time management:

KNOW WHAT YOU WANT TO DO AND DON'T FORGET IT.

You can use your memory to get the most out of your day and maintain a constant awareness of the necessity for time management. The first step is to recognize what interferes with what you want to do.

GETTING RID OF TIME WASTERS

Here is a list of ten common time wasters. Consider them all, acknowledge them, and if any apply to you, *memorize* them.

Armed with knowledge, you'll be able to defend yourself from their encroachment. Your awareness of them will act as an automatic pilot to keep you on course.

1. Interruptions
2. Telephone calls
3. Visitors
4. Waiting
5. Meetings
6. Slow start in the morning
7. Personal conversations
8. Lack of deadlines
9. Inability to say no
10. Coffee breaks (it's been said we spend twenty-two days a year on them)

Using Memory Blueprint 3 (Rhyming Words), memorize the time wasters you want to avoid. Repeat them three times a day and you're on your way to controlling your use of time.

With your picture for:

Gun,	associate	Interruptions.
Shoe,	associate	Telephone
Tree,	associate	Visitors
Door,	associate	Waiting
Dive,	associate	Meeting
Sticks,	associate	Slow start
Heaven,	associate	Personal conversations
Gate,	associate	Deadlines
Wine,	associate	Say no
Hen,	associate	Coffee breaks

SETTING PRIORITIES

One of the most effective time-management tools is a daily priority list of what you want to accomplish. Late each day set up your priority list for the next day. Then select a memory blueprint to help you memorize it. On your way home run it through your mind a couple of times, and then go on with your usual evening routine. By the end of the evening you will have planted the seed in the sleepless servant of your subconscious mind. You'll be surprised at how you'll hit the ground running the next day.

With that list firmly in your memory, you can handle interruptions easily. Suppose your boss approaches and says, "Stop what you're doing and take care of this." You can say, "OK. I have six items on my priority list for today and I've already done three. I can put this ahead of the others." Or you could ask, "OK I have six things to do for today. Do you want me to make this number one or can it wait a bit?"

Or suppose a colleague is trying to involve you in her responsibilities. Instead of saying no outright, you might say to yourself, "Turn it over to **LeNoRA.**" Who's Lenora?

L *isten.*
N *o.* Politely and pleasantly, say no.
R *easons.* Explain the reasons why you can't agree.
A *lternatives.* Suggest some alternatives for solving her problems.

These two memory methods—memorizing time wasters and creating a daily priority list—will take care of most of your time-management problems. With them in mind every day, you'll remind yourself to consult other methods that will help you change your surroundings and procedures for better time management.

REMEMBERING YOUR GOALS

In any seminar program or book on time management, you will find many checklists that you will use only occasionally, when a special need arises: a list of forty principles of time management, twelve suggestions on dealing with interruptions, ten tips for organizing your work area, twenty ideas for crisis management, five ways to cut down on correspondence and paper work. You'll review these lists and, in many cases, put the advice immediately into practice. But you don't need to commit them *all* to memory, because you may not use them all. However, some of the ideas may strike a chord with you, and you'll want to make sure you remember them by using an appropriate memory blueprint. For instance, out of the checklist of forty time-manage-

ment principles, you might decide on three goals that require
your constant awareness:

> **R** *eading* speed
> **C** *onference calls*
> **A** *ccumulated* telephone calls

You can make a jogger from the initials: **RCA** or **CAR.**
    Here's another example: A bank president I know took a sem-
inar on time management, making extensive notes. Later he nar-
rowed them down to ten things he was going to do to improve
his own time management. (I have emphasized the key words
in each.)

1. Redistribute *mail* including systems for sorting training
   material, economic information, regulations, and routine
   payments.
2. Allocate time for visits to *department heads*, branches, and
   customers.
3. Have a summary of *large accounts* and big movements.
4. Program *customer calls.*
5. Handle *contributions.*
6. Financial *charts.*
7. New-employee *training.*
8. *Treasury* plan—evaluation, courses, seminars.
9. No *briefcase* taken home.
10. Start *on time.*

He planned to go over this list regularly, with a thorough review, but found that many things interfered. I suggested that
instead of worrying about being interrupted, he put his energy
into memorizing the ten items. I asked him to underline the key
word in each point and then, using Memory Blueprint 2 in a
slightly expanded form, to arrange pictorial clues in a setting
that would remind him to do the review.
    He started by picturing himself sitting at his desk. At his right
he placed a pictorial clue that to him represented **MAIL,** and in
front of him a clue for **DEPARTMENT HEADS.** He placed his
other clues to his left, behind him, under his feet, and over his
head. That took care of six. He placed the seventh clue across

the desk in front of him, the eighth coming through the doorway, the ninth on the front wall of his office, and the tenth on the face of his office clock.

HELPING OTHERS MANAGE THEIR TIME

If you manage a staff of people, you can increase their productivity by helping them to be more efficient with their time. Start by asking yourself eight questions:

1. Are staff members keeping time logs?
2. What problems do the logs reveal?
3. Who or what is responsible for the problems?
4. Are the staff prioritizing work? What are the priorities of the problems?
5. What action needs to be taken now?
6. What time-management techniques can be applied?
7. What schedules or guides can be set up?
8. What steps should I take to follow up?

Now the idea is to remember them all! List the key words in the eight questions:

1. *log*
2. *problems*
3. *responsibility*
4. *priorities*
5. *action*
6. *techniques*
7. *schedules*
8. *follow up*

Let's see how you could use various memory blueprints to process these points into your memory bank. Using Memory Blueprint 9 (The Cementing Sentence), I come up with: **LOG PROBLEMS** of **RESPONSIBILITY PRIORITIES** and **ACTION TECHNIQUES** for **SCHEDULE FOLLOW-UP.**
Memory Blueprint 3 (Rhyming Words) provides a pictorial display. You can associate:

"Gun" with *log*
"Shoe" with *problems*
"Tree" with *responsibility*
"Door" with *priorities*
"Dive" with *action*
"Sticks" with *techniques*
"Heaven" with *schedules*
"Gate" with *follow-up*

Or you can use Memory Blueprint 6 (The Shoehorn Sentence). Here is an example: **Let's Pray Real Profits Are Tomorrow's Salvation Finally.**

As a manager, one of your most critical tasks is to heighten your staff's motivation. Believe it or not, you can put memory joggers to good use even here. For example, many people resist keeping daily logs; it seems like drudgery to them. Try this. Say: "Look at it this way. A **LOG** helps me in:

"**L** ocating
"**O** ptimum
"**G** ains"

With a light touch, you've encouraged that person to see that keeping a log is important—and helped her remember why.

USING YOUR MEMORY TO SAVE TIME

Did you ever stop to think how much time you waste looking things up? Or how much time is lost when critical directions are misunderstood or forgotten? Have you ever missed an important meeting because you didn't write it on your calendar—or forgot to *look* at your calendar? Then how much time did you have to invest to catch up?

Here's where your good memory is worth a fortune to you. With appointments, instructions, and other critical information in the front of your mind, you'll never use good productive time searching for that information.

Remembering Appointments. Of course, paper and pencil play a role in remembering appointments and schedules. But it is useful to include your appointments for the next few days or a week on your memory list of daily priorities. This doesn't apply to professionals and executives with busy and tight schedules. They need a good appointment book and a conscientious secretary to keep track of things. However, for most people with relatively few appointments, the priority list is a good place to store tomorrow's appointments.

Remembering Important Occasions. You can do impressive things with your memory for items on your future schedule. Perhaps you'll want to show your interest in another person by remembering an anniversary or a birthday. They're easy to remember. Most of us have pictures for each month—a heart for February, a turkey for November. You can use them to fix a date in your mind.

For instance, let's assume John's anniversary is the third of November. Imagine giving him three turkeys. Say your boss's birthday is the twenty-first of December; you might imagine that you are presenting her with a 21-foot Christmas tree.

Following Instructions. Since misunderstanding instructions wastes time, step-by-step instructions for operations on the job lend themselves readily to the use of memory blueprints. Do you know the saying "If the worker hasn't learned, the instructor hasn't taught"? It's harsh but true. Both worker and instructor should use memory blueprints to guarantee that every step is covered and in the right order. Memory Blueprint 1 (Initial Letters) or Memory Blueprint 6 (The Shoehorn Sentence) can be helpful in making sure you remember instructions—quickly.

Remembering Directions. Recalling directions accurately is a great time saver. Any businessperson who is always on the road with lots of appointments knows that. Memory Blueprint 7 (The Chain) adapts easily to travel directions. For instance, say you're being given directions over a car phone while driving:

"Take Main Street to I-495." See yourself paying a $4.95 toll to get off Main Street.

"Take I-495 to the turnpike, Route I-90 west." Picture yourself driving ninety miles an hour on the turnpike.

"Take Route 20 exit at Syracuse and you'll see the plant right off the ramp." Imagine twenty men from Syracuse University blocking the turnpike.

Using memory blueprints will help you pay constant attention to the key question, "How do I spend my time?" With judicious use of your memory, every hour will be **PRIME TIME:**

P restige
R esourcefulness
I ncome
M ore popularity
E ffectiveness

T hrough
I ncreased
M ental
E nergy

7

Getting the Most Out Of Business Reading

You are probably only too well aware of the problems of handling business reading. Maybe you have developed methods of processing the routine flow of material generated internally by your company. Of course, the most difficult reading is that which is extended, serious, and slowgoing. Memory blueprints can lead you through that maze of business reading to effective comprehension, application, and recognition.

HOW TO REMEMBER WHAT YOU READ

The following eight steps will help you increase your retention and cut down the time necessary to thoroughly absorb new pertinent information:

1. *Skim* the material. Look over the table of contents, paragraph headings, and the first line of each paragraph for an idea of overall content.
2. *Underline* the significant points in each paragraph.
3. *Express* the content of that paragraph or significant section *in your own words.* At this point, you have already cut your learning time in half by consciously assimilating the material into your own thought patterns.

You can remember these three steps by using the memory jogger **SUE:**

> **S** kim
> **U** nderline
> **E** xpress

4. Create a *headline* for each paragraph.
5. Write down the *initial* letters of your headlines. Consider their use as a memory blueprint.
6. Make a mental *picture* of the headline for use in other types of blueprints.

Remember these three steps with the memory jogger **HIP.**

H eadline
I nitial
P icture

7. *Memorize* the points held by your blueprint.
8. *Repeat* the material, using the blueprints.

The complete memory jogger for business reading is **SUE HIP MR.** Let's see how you can apply this blueprint to an article on performance review. Say your objective is to understand its contents so thoroughly that you can present the procedure without notes at a management meeting. I think you'll find it easiest to work on the first four steps as a block:

1. Skim the entire article.
2. Underline key words.
3. Express the gist of each paragraph in a few words.
4. Create a headline for each paragraph.

Let's see how it works out.

PERFORMANCE REVIEW

People in supervision should periodically compare the performance of individuals under their direction with the standards of performance that have been established. This requires the ability to tell people exactly what you think of their performance and still command their respect and confidence.

Your summary of the previous paragraph could be just five words: "Tell it like it is."

Your headline word: "tell."

Now do the second paragraph:

> This is the most difficult phase of supervision. It is the point at which managers and supervisors analyze the performance of their organization as <u>compared with the standards</u> of performance.

Summary: "Must be based on standards."
Headline: "standards."

Now the third paragraph:

> This is the point at which <u>problem cases</u> must be squarely faced. Management cannot and dare not evade individual problem cases. Leaders who have the capacity to discuss the performance of individuals with those individuals themselves have few so-called problem cases in their organization.

Summary and headline: "problem cases."

The fourth paragraph:

> When periodic checking of complete performance is advocated, the reaction is often expressed that "we are continually checking performance." Current checking always has been done and is being done. This management plan makes a major contribution in providing for a review of complete performance at definite intervals so that the employee may see his own <u>balance sheet.</u>

Summary: "Complete review yields balance sheet."
Headline: "balance sheet."

The fifth paragraph:

> A discussion between supervisor and employee at the time of failure is not always sound. Such a discussion may be

subject to the <u>emotions</u> of the moment and when emotions enter, reason exits.

Summary and headline: "emotions."

The sixth paragraph:

Another value of periodic performance review is that it provides an opportunity for <u>commendation</u> as well as <u>condemnation</u>.[1]

Summary: "Balance praise and blame."
Headline: "praise."

Here's a list of the headline words for those six paragraphs:

1. *tell*
2. *standards*
3. *problem cases*
4. *balance sheet*
5. *emotions*
6. *praise*

We have now covered the first four steps of

S kim
U nderline
E xpress

and

H eadline

Now let's find a memory blueprint to help us remember the six points. The next two steps are:

I nitial
P icture

---

1. From "A Program of Organization and Management," reprinted by permission of Mobil Oil Corporation.

That is, look over the six points and see what kind of memory blueprint works better here: one based on initial letters or one based on mental pictures?

First let's see if the initials of the six headlines make a memory blueprint. They do. Using Memory Blueprint 6 (The Shoehorn Sentence), I come up with **T**ell **S**ome **P**recocious **B**eginners **E**xtra **P**raise. This shoehorn sentence has the advantage of using two of the actual headline words. In fact, this list of six headlines makes a straightforward cementing sentence (Memory Blueprint 9): **TELL STANDARD PROBLEMS** and **BALANCE EMOTIONS** with **PRAISE.**

But sometimes you just can't do anything with the initials of your headlines, so you look at the pictorial possibilities. Let's follow on with our example, to illustrate the full process. What can we do with the pictures these six headline words represent?

We could put them in six spaces around our body (that's Memory Blueprint 2). We could locate them in six spots in our house (Memory Blueprint 4). Let's see what we can do with Memory Blueprint 3 (Rhyming Words). Remember:

One = "gun."
Two = "shoe."
Three = "tree."
Four = "door."
Five = "dive."
Six = "sticks."

Just a reminder: It is not necessary to have a logical connection between the words forming your blueprint and the key words that you are visualizing. Any *pictorial* association that you can make between *your* picture for "gun" and *your* picture for the first point, "tell," will make it stick.

One = "gun."	Make a pictorial association with "tell."
Two = "shoe."	Make a pictorial association with "standards."
Three = "tree."	Make a pictorial association with "problem cases."
Four = "door."	Make a pictorial association with "balance sheet."

Five = "dive."   Make a pictorial association with "emotions."
Six = "sticks."   Make a pictorial association with "praise."

The list of six items might be a good place to try Memory Blueprint 5 (The Alphabet). Make pictorial associations between the blueprint words:

Ape   _____

Bee   _____

Cedar   _____

Deed   _____

Eel   _____

Fox   _____

Remember Memory Blueprint 10 (Your Individual Creation)? Before moving on, let me show you how I used my interest in baseball to make pictorial associations with the six points in the article on performance review. I'll use the players in the order in which I think of them. Here is my blueprint and the headline I associate with each. You, of course, will make your own pictorial association.

Pitcher = "tell."
Catcher = "standards."
First base = "problem cases."
Second base = "balance sheet."
Shortstop = "emotions."
Third base = "praise."

There remains only the third portion of the memory jogger. Then the process is complete:

M emorize
R epeat

FOLLOWING THE RECIPE

Is it digestible? A batch of cookie dough is not in digestible condition. However, if you cook it at 350 degrees for fifteen minutes you will have made it easy to handle, delicious to eat, and easy to digest. If you're in a hurry, it won't do to raise the oven to 550 degrees and cook the dough for less time. Determine your own timetable to ready new information for mental digestion.

You must memorize and repeat the thoughts associated with the headlines until you've mastered the procedures involved in a performance review and feel comfortable explaining them at a meeting.

HOW TO MASTER A SELF-IMPROVEMENT BOOK

Because of the way they are organized, self-improvement books present a special opportunity to quickly establish the main points in your memory before reading the entire book. Most of these books summarize their main points in the first chapter. Subsequent chapters amplify the basic principles and show how to apply them. If you memorize those key points first, you will have an efficient outline with which to more quickly benefit from what follows.

Here is a useful example: Early in their book, *Success Through a Positive Mental Attitude*, Napoleon Hill and W. Clement Stone write:

> As long as you live, from this day forward, you can analyze your every success and every failure—that is if you imprint these 17 principles indelibly in your memory.
>
> You may develop and maintain a permanent Positive Mental Attitude by making it your responsibility to adopt and apply these 17 principles to your daily living. *There is no other known method by which you can keep your mind positive.*[2]

2. Englewood Cliffs, N.J.: Prentice-Hall, 1988. Reprinted by permission of the publisher.

To imprint those seventeen principles indelibly in your mind, use Memory Blueprint 1 (Initial Letters). Since it isn't necessary to remember the seventeen items in any particular order, you can rearrange them so that the initial letters spell words for a memory jogger.

This is how I did it. I listed the seventeen principles in the order given in the book as follows:

1. A positive mental attitude
2. Definiteness of purpose
3. Going the extra mile
4. Accurate thinking
5. Self-discipline
6. The mastermind
7. Applied faith
8. A pleasing personality
9. Personal initiative
10. Enthusiasm
11. Controlled attention
12. Teamwork
13. Learning from defeat
14. Creative vision
15. Budgeting time and money
16. Maintaining sound physical and mental health
17. Using cosmic habit force (universal law)[3]

I selected these key words:

positive
definite
extra mile
accurate thinking
self-discipline
mastermind
applied faith
personality
initiative

3. Adapted from Hill and Stone, *op. cit.*

enthusiasm
attention (controlled)
teamwork
defeat
creative
budgeting
health
universal

Then I listed the initial letters of the key words:

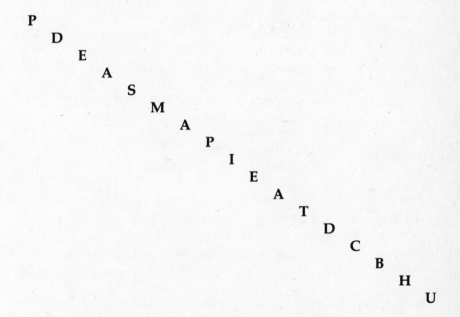

As I looked down this list of initials for Memory Blueprint 1 possibilities, **PEAS** jumped out at me. Then I saw **MAP.** Next came **IEA**; with the D left over from the second principle, that made **IDEA.** The remaining six letters were rearranged to form **B DUTCH.**

Note: When you are making up your own Memory Blueprint 1 (Initial Letters), you will find it helpful to choose key words beginning with vowels. This makes it easier to construct meaningful words.

Here is my complete memory jogger for the seventeen principles for success:

1. **P** ositive mental attitude
2. **E** xtra mile
3. **A** ccurate thinking
4. **S** elf-discipline

5. **M** astermind
6. **A** pplied faith
7. **P** leasing personality

8. **I** nitiative
9. **D** efinite purpose
10. **E** nthusiasm
11. **A** ttention (controlled)

12. **B** udgeting time and money

13. **D** efeat (learning from)
14. **U** niversal law
15. **T** eamwork
16. **C** reative vision
17. **H** ealth

The initials provide an easily remembered memory jogger: **PEAS
MAP IDEA B DUTCH.** Use this to carry these powerful principles in your conscious mind. Incidentally, a recent book[4] has
reexamined the application of these principles to current business practice, and finds them still basic and sound after thirty
years.

Dale Carnegie's classic, *How to Win Friends and Influence People,*[5] contains a total of thirty-four basic rules in groups of six,
seven, nine, and twelve. These are summarized at the end of
each section. I'm sure you can create your own memory jogger
to implant these powerful ideas in your mind.

The next time you start to read a self-help book, skim it first,
look for the fundamental rules or principles, and create memory

---

4. Samuel Cypert, *Believe and Achieve: W. Clement Stone's New Success Formula* (New York:
Dodd, 1988).
5. New York: Pocket Books, 1983.

blueprints so that you can learn them and keep them in your permanent memory.

SPEED READING TO HELP YOU REMEMBER MORE

Businesspeople need to be familiar with all aspects of an issue before making a decision. Speed reading is one way to gain the broader view of a topic *and* increase your retention. When you increase your reading speed, you automatically remember more from the mountain of reading material facing you.

You can teach yourself to read faster. Clear the way with a kitchen timer. Set it for thirty seconds. Pick up a book and read it with a drive for speed until the timer goes off. Then try to repeat out loud as much as you remember from what you just read. Don't worry if you missed something. Try again for thirty seconds with a different section. Always drive for speed! The fact that you missed something will heighten your resolve to concentrate better the next time.

When you are satisfied with your ability to do well for thirty seconds, try for sixty. Keep stretching the time as your skill in retention at maximum speed increases. The timer is essential. It keeps you from wondering if the time is up, so you can concentrate fully on what you're reading.

This method works because you automatically concentrate better when you are driving for speed. If you leisurely row a boat across a river, you will be diverted by the current and bump into whatever is floating in your path. However, if you put a motor on the boat, the speed will set up a bow wave that will throw the floating debris away from the boat and enable you to cross the river in a straight line in spite of the current.

Remember, when you drive for speed in reading, you are automatically increasing your concentration and memory for what you read.

REAPING REWARDS FROM READING

Applying memory blueprints to your business reading can also discreetly increase your visibility at work. Here's how. Suppose

---

ARE YOU IN A BOX?

Do your associates have fixed opinions about your ability and capacity that you would like to change? Have you ever thought that others may be thinking, "He's a good worker but . . ." or "Well, we all know what Joan is like . . ."? You can break out of the box! Make a concerted effort to do two things: Use memory methods in listening, and make constructive and well-organized suggestions based on business reading, contacts, seminars, and other sources. I guarantee your associates will have a new estimate of your abilities.

---

you read an article that lists six steps to improve your company's security. Using the memory blueprint of your choice, you can memorize the six steps. Then walk into your boss's office and say, "I just read an article on how to improve our security. It pinpoints six particular actions, such as. . . ." and recount them from memory. Then say, "I thought you might like a copy."

In other words, don't merely give your boss a copy of the article and say, "You might want to read this." That can easily backfire! She might say thank-you, but she could be thinking, "Good grief, when am I going to get time to read this? I wish he wouldn't keep dumping stuff on my desk."

Instead, verbally present the information and then hand her the written material. You have brought to your boss's attention the fact that you are not only keeping track of important information but are applying it and offering something to the company.

8

Profiting From Seminars

Myself when young did eagerly frequent
Doctor and Saint, and heard great argument
About it and about: but evermore
Came out by the same door wherein I went.

—Omar Khayyam

I think Omar must have attended a lot of seminars.

In training, nothing happens until somebody remembers something. Do you remember every important point made at the last seminar you attended? Is each so clearly registered in your mind that you can habitually use it? Can you write down right now why you attended and just exactly what you gained from that seminar? Has the seminar made a measurable contribution to your personal effectiveness and your company's profit?

If you had doubts about answering yes to any of those questions, then perhaps it's time to devote thought to deliberately cultivating new habits. Using memory blueprints will help you leave the next seminar or group meeting feeling certain that you know what was said, why it was said, and how you can work it into the mainstream of your useful business knowledge, use it, and get credit for it!

Major Kenneth Rogers was the executive officer at an army installation where I was conducting a class on memory for civilians. He had scheduled the course but was skeptical. At dinner I soon had him recalling so many items that he'd thought he never could remember that he became one of my most enthusiastic supporters.

A few months later he was transferred to a staff school, and there he hit the jackpot. He phoned to tell me that he was using my methods to summarize the points covered in weekly seminars. He was the only one doing it from memory! I don't know how high up in the command he has gone since, but I wouldn't be surprised if he has stars on his shoulders!

Seminars are often faulted for offering either too little or too much information, and a lot of time and money are on the line when we attend them. When they offer too much I liken it to having groceries for a year dumped on your front lawn. You would have to store the food, take out a little at a time, prepare it, and eat it in reasonably sized meals.

It is possible, however, to take the information offered, store it, select the portions you wish to master, and systematically apply memory tools to their complete and personally profitable absorption.

MAKING SENSE OF SEMINARS

Memory Blueprint 1 is great for preparing for and participating in a seminar. In fact the blueprint spells **SEMINAR:**

S   *can* announcement.
E   *stablish* interest and questions.
M   *ark* key answers you expect to secure.
I   *nitiate* questions.
N   *otes.*
A   *ccumulate* key points and review.
R   *ecord.*

This memory jogger will remind you of seven preparatory steps.

1. Before you attend your next seminar *scan* the announcement and the list of objectives.
2. Think over what is of *greatest interest* to you and frame questions about it.
3. Be prepared in advance; *mark questions* you want answered.
4. When the session is open for participants' questions, have at least one pertinent *question* ready.
5. Take good *notes*—but not too many!
6. Accumulate a list of *key points,* and at every break do a quick visual *review.*
7. As soon as possible after the session, dictate your summary into a *tape recorder.*

You have now opened a mental bank account of information from which you can draw valuable new ideas and procedures. With the equity in that account, you won't react as some do who attend seminars: "I feel that if I can pick up one or two good ideas, it's been worth the money." That's like saying, "They were offering me a bucket of ten-dollar gold pieces, and I only brought a tin cup!" We have all seen seminar ads that promise, "You will learn. . . ." followed by a list of twenty or thirty items. Blueprints will convert your exposure into significant results.

When you return from a seminar, your boss is bound to ask you how it went. If you analyze and memorize the main points in one key section, you can reply, "It was great! Just loaded with good information. There was one section about . . . that made the following points: . . ." Then provide the information from memory. I guarantee that your boss will be glad he sent *you*.

INTENSE SEMINAR SUBJECTS

One reason seminars have a bad reputation in some circles is that some people have the impression they all deal with "soft" subjects: "Creative Problem Solving," "Stress Management in the Workplace," "Goal Setting and Peak Performance." Don't get me wrong: I am one who believes these kinds of topics are extremely relevant for good managers today. The point is that not all seminars are like this; some are intense presentations of complex subject matter, perhaps involving several "classes" over a period of time. We might compare them to graduate-level academic seminars, for they require the same kind of concentration and study by the participants.

To thoroughly master material in these more complex seminars, tackle the material systematically. Combine your favorite memory blueprint with this nine-step plan.

1. Set up a headline word, a clue word, for each significant point. Refer to Chapter 7 ("Business Reading") for instructions on determining and constructing clues.
2. Memorize twenty headlines, using your memory blueprint. Think about them repeatedly in the time your blueprint provides.

3. Review the material at least three times a day—at mealtime, while commuting, just before falling asleep. At the end of three days, those twenty points should be well established in your permanent body of knowledge.
4. List the headline words in writing.
5. Read the list onto an audiocassette, leaving a space after each word. Review the tape often; in the blank spaces, check your recollection of the material associated with each headline.
6. Use the same memory blueprint to memorize and review the next twenty headlines.
7. For three days proceed as you did with the first twenty.
8. Read over the written list of the *first* twenty headlines, checking for any that need reinforcement in your memory. Add the latest twenty to your cassette. Play it occasionally for speedy, complete review of the subject to that point.
9. Continue this series of steps every time you complete the three-day review of twenty points. Read over the entire list of preceding headlines and play the cassette as convenient. You could probably review 200 headlines in an hour.

MAKING THE MOST OF CONTACTS

The people you meet at seminars are sometimes as important as the information provided—maybe more so. I'm sure you have found yourself, months after a seminar, trying to conjure up a name, a company, even an image of an attendee who had indicated interest in your company. From now on, you can prepare for remembering people you meet—and forever cease that "groping." Just follow these three simple steps:

1. Ask people for their business cards.
2. Write down information about them on the cards.
3. Back at the office prepare a detailed list for future use.

Since your memory is under a heavy load at a seminar, use it wisely. Keep notes on people, and memorize the significant information about them as soon as possible. There's more on remembering people—their faces and names—in Chapter 4.

If the information offered in a seminar overwhelms your natural retentive ability, you lose and your company loses. We all have to take every intelligent step available to increase our effectiveness and bring essential information to the cutting edge of profitable action. By applying the preceding memory techniques when you attend your next seminar, you will derive three important benefits:

1. An orderly procedure for working the new information into your body of business knowledge
2. Sharpened skills that supply leverage in any learning situation
3. Recognition and reward for applying your newly acquired knowledge in your daily business activities

9

Enhancing Your Sales and Persuasion Techniques

In business nothing happens until somebody sells something.
—RED MOTLEY, former publisher of *Parade* Magazine

Listening attentively to hot sales-generating techniques is one thing. Remembering them well enough to use them is another. How often have you thought, after hearing one of the many masterful presentations on some aspect of sales practice such as closing the sale or overcoming objections, "If I could only remember half of what that speaker said, I could double my sales!"

LESSONS FROM SEVEN MASTERS

Robert Louis Stevenson wrote, "Every man lives by selling something." Because of that statement, Zenn Kaufman, a great sales trainer, chose Stevenson as one of his seven historical "masters of marketing." Zenn illustrated several selling strategies and made his points memorable by using the sayings of famous people. Here are the other six masters, and the lessons in selling we all can learn from them:

- Zsa Zsa Gabor: "Men are like fires; they go out unless attended to."
  Lesson: Keep in touch with your customers.

- Willy Sutton, when asked why he robbed banks: "Because that's where the money is."
  Lesson: Be sure your prospect is financially qualified.
- Cato, the Roman emperor, at the end of every speech: "Carthage must be destroyed." And eventually it was.
  Lesson: Repetition wins the day.
- Bert Williams, songwriter: "Everybody Wants to Go to Heaven But Nobody Wants to Die."
  Lesson: Do everything necessary to make the sale.
- Benjamin Disraeli: "Take your job seriously, but not yourself."
  Lesson: self-evident.
- Daniel Defoe: "Let not thine apprentice run thy shop. The customer wants to hear the master's voice."
  Lesson: Don't delegate essential customer contacts as you move up.

The use of famous names is an effective device. Haven't you noticed how television uses well-known people to attract attention and increase believability? If the President, a famous sports star, or your favorite TV actor told you something in private, would you ever forget it? Now you try it: Vividly imagine a celebrity telling you an important piece of information! It's a fascinating way to reinforce your memory.

CLOSING A SALE

One of the most dynamic sales trainers I ever met was J. Douglas Edwards. His presentations were solid, straightforward, and practical. At the end of one of his talks covering thirteen ways to close a sale, he said, "Now we've had some fun and I've yelled at you, but only two or three of you in this audience will go out and do what is necessary to follow my instructions. These techniques must be learned, *and that takes time!"*

Edwards was right—it does take time. But if you use the memory blueprints and the techniques you have learned so far, it will take you less time than it takes most people.

In Chapter 2, I show how to use Memory Blueprint 6 (The

Shoehorn Sentence) to remember Edwards's seven-point procedure for handling a final objection. The points had to be remembered in order but the thirteen closes do not. You can use Memory
Blueprint 1 to arrange the initial letters into meaningful and
therefore easily remembered words.

Here's my arrangement. The memory jogger is **FAST BOSS
SCALP.**

F   *inal objection.*
A   *lternate choice.* Ask *which,* not *what.*
S   *ummary close.* Add up the benefits.
T   *hink it over.* Ask what he wants to think over, and summarize
the benefits.

B   *alance sheet.* Ben Franklin's favorite.
O   *rder blank.* Just start filling it in.
S   *imilar situation.* Someone who had the same problem.
S   *tory close.* Of someone who decided favorably.

S   *econdary question.* One that implies consent to the sale.
C   *all back.* "I may have forgotten to mention that. . . ."
A   *ngle (sharp).* "If it comes in red, do you want it?"
L   *ost sales close.* "Help me! Tell me what I missed."
P   *uppy dog close.* "When a pet shop lets you take a puppy home,
you're bound to buy it. Give your prospect a trial period."

If you memorize these key words and review the aspects of
closing that they represent three times a day for three days, the
techniques will become a useful and profitable part of your sales
knowledge.

THINKING ON YOUR FEET

I frequently address groups of salespeople in various fields. Before my presentation, I try to chat informally with several people, and have found that very few of them—and these are
professional salespeople—can say right off the bat what is special about their product. Thinking on your feet is important in
sales. And using memory joggers is a powerful way of enhancing that ability.

For example, you may sell real estate. Ask yourself, What are twelve reasons someone would want to list a house with me? Now create a memory jogger to remember them. Here are twelve reasons I can think of—and a memory jogger to remember them by: **AVID FOIL PASS.**

A   ttention
V   alue
I   nformation
D   eposit

F   inancing
O   pen house
I   nside (showing inside of house, not just exterior)
L   egal arrangements

P   rice
A   dvertising
S   ales force
S   igns

USING CASSETTES TO ENHANCE YOUR MEMORY

A tremendous amount of useful material on selling is available on cassettes, which salespeople can take advantage of. For instance, Dick Palmer, of Palmer Tire in Macon, Georgia, one of the top tire distributors in the United States, has his salespeople constantly play professional sales tapes while driving. The success of his company proves that listening and spaced repetition do work, despite the pressures of time and the distractions of traffic.

Before working with a cassette in the car, I suggest that you listen to it first at home or in the office. Make notes of the major points and use one of the memory blueprints to memorize them. Then use your driving time for reviewing and mastering the material.

HOW TO BE WELCOME EVERY TIME YOU WALK IN

You will have a tremendous advantage in any selling situation if you prepare yourself in advance with information about the other people involved and have a plan for your presentation. Chapter 4 shows you how to accumulate advance information about people and their interests. Here's another winning idea.

Successful salespeople are achievers because they habitually look for new ideas to help their customers. As you know, newsletters are a great source of this type of information. *Boardroom Reports* and *The Bottom Line* are both gold mines of ideas. But rather than offer a photocopy from a page of these newsletters, use your memory blueprints to memorize the ideas themselves. Then when you walk into the office of a customer or a prospect, you can say, "I came across an idea in *Boardroom Reports* that I thought might interest you. It said. . . ." and then explain it from memory. Let your customer see what a good memory you have, and how intelligently you are using it for her benefit. Not only will you walk in a winner, but you will greatly increase your chances of walking out with a sale.

BUILDING A VOCABULARY OF SALES WORDS

Professional salespeople are masters of the tools of persuasion—words. They cultivate and make use of carefully selected power words in their conversation. Dave Yoho, one of the great sales trainers, has a list of forty power words and phrases. Let's look at them and then see what steps you can take to make using them habitual.

assurance	*help*
confidence	*I appreciate*
courtesy	*I understand*
durable	*love*
enjoyment	*modern*
easy	*money*
expert	*necessary*
fun	*new*
growth	*original*
guarantee	*peace of mind*
health	*popular*

prestige	*security*
pride	*service*
profitable	*share*
protection	*stimulating*
proven	*stylish*
quality	*thank you for*
relief	*unexcelled*
results	*you*
save	*your*

It's a formidable list. But see how easy it is to organize those words into simple memory joggers. You can readily make up words from the initials of these words even though there are a limited number of vowels available. We all want **SUCCESS,** so let's start with:

S ervice
U nexcelled
C ourtesy
C onfidence
E njoyment
S tylish
S timulating

That's enough for one mental meal. The next step is to memorize these seven words and then *force* them into your sales vocabulary over a period of several days. When you have made them part of your normal usage, pick up another group. But remember, you must take a few words at a time and feed them into your regular dialogue systematically. Take a week to learn small groups of words. Now let's meet **MRS. Gee Gee** and **MR. POPE.**

M odern
R elief
S hare

G rowth
G uarantee

M oney
R esults

P restige
O riginal
P rotection
E asy

You're on your own for the other twenty-two power words. In about four weeks conduct a complete review of your sales conversation, and you'll see how these powerful words have become part of your vocabulary.

MAKING YOURSELF AND YOUR WORDS MEMORABLE

Throughout this book, I've talked about ways *you* can remember things, principally through the use of creative memory joggers. But sometimes you want your *customers* to remember something. You can use the same techniques to reinforce in their mind the key selling messages you want to leave with them.

I have sold millions of dollars' worth of mutual funds because I deliberately set up my sales points on a word easily remembered by my prospects, many of whom did not buy on the first call and all of whom would probably have asked advice from someone else. Here is what I said: "In every investment decision you have to think of **SIAM.** That stands for:

S afety. How safe is it in terms of dollars and purchasing power?
I nterest. Return on investment.
A ppreciation. Growth in value.
M arketability. How fast can I get my money?"

I was able to plant those points so firmly in my prospects' memory that I warded off competitors. My prospects became my customers because they saw sound advice in **SIAM** and knew that that advice came from me.

Create your own memory jogger slogan and watch the results!

10

Becoming An Effective Public Speaker

Do you consider making a speech a fate worse than death? You're not alone! Many people fear public speaking, but there are ways to overcome this fear—and to become a good speaker. Memory blueprints can help you remember the rules for organizing your talk, keep you from forgetting what you want to say, and provide the means for making your speech memorable to your audience.

SIX RULES FOR EXCELLENCE

Everything we know about competent speechmaking can be boiled down to six rules. Learn them, apply them, and you'll be on your way. Here are the rules:

1. Know your subject.
2. Organize your talk.
3. Remember what you planned to say.
4. Make your audience remember.
5. Use an authoritative voice.
6. Speak clearly.

Rule 1: Know Your Subject. The first rule in public speaking is to know what you're talking about. If you don't, you have a right to be nervous! If you do know, and if you can remember what you want to say, you may still have butterflies in your stomach, but at least you can train them to fly in formation!

Rule 2: Organize Your Talk. Because you know about memory joggers, if you organize your talk properly (rule 2), you'll have no problem remembering what you want to say (rule 3). They really go hand in hand. Your best tactic is to organize your key points in such a way that they naturally fit into a memory blueprint; that way, remembering them is a snap.

At the same time, there is a general structure, an overall skeleton, that you can use for almost any public speaking situation. Whenever you make any sort of speech, you want your audience to do something as a result of having heard you. To lead them toward this action point, fit your speech into this five-step structure:

1. **A**   ttention
2. **P**   oint
3. **R**   easons
4. **E**   xamples
5. **S**   o what

Yes, you're absolutely right; there's a memory jogger here: **A PRES,** short for *"a pres*entation." A presentation should be organized along these lines:

1. Grab your audience's *attention* with a question or a startling statement.
2. Establish your *points.*
3. Provide *reasons* supporting your points.
4. Offer *examples* to illustrate your points.
5. Your listeners should be wondering, *"So what* does this speaker expect me to do now?" Make sure you give them an answer! Appeal for an action they can take immediately.

A talk I gave to Rotary clubs in support of a program for wiping out polio worldwide illustrates these five steps.

1. *Attention.* "If I could promise you that you could save the lives of eight children for just one dollar before you leave this room, how many of you would give me a dollar?" (I put up my hand to encourage them to put up theirs.)

2. *Point.* "For just one dollar you can supply enough polio vaccine to inoculate eight children, children who will otherwise die or be condemned to spend their lives as beggars."

3. *Reasons.* "We Rotarians have joined forces with The United Nations Children's Fund and The World Health Organization to eliminate polio throughout the world in just six years!"

4. *Examples.* "Polio has practically disappeared from the Dominican Republic. We have already cut the polio rate in the Philippines by sixty percent. This program will save in ten years more lives than have been lost in all the wars of history!"

5. *So what?* "You don't have to give a dollar. You can give more! Ten dollars will save eighty children. I've named a captain at every table. Let's see how many productive lives we can save today! Dig deep and give. You'll never make a better gift!"

Rule 3: Remember What You Planned to Say. The basic fear in public speaking is that your nervousness will cause you to forget. There's a simple way to avoid being bombed out by the butterflies: Arrange your points in order based on a memory blueprint—which is rule 2. If you do that, then rule 3 is a snap. But if for some reason you don't, or can't, follow a blueprint at the organizing stage, do it now. List your key points in headline form, and then look over the list to see which memory blueprint fits best. Memorize your blueprint, and step up to the podium self-confidently.

Rule 4: Make Your Audience Remember. Of course you must remember what you want to say; equally important, you must make sure your audience remembers what you say. How many times have you enthusiastically applauded a terrific speech—and then realized the next day that you couldn't remember the talk well enough to derive any real benefit from it?

What can you, as the speaker, do about it? What works for me is to provide memory joggers for the key points in my presentations. I have my audience repeat my joggers and adopt the blueprint as their own.

For instance, say you are presenting a new product and want to discuss the **M**arketing, **A**dvertising, and **P**roduction of it. You can begin by saying, "I'm going to show you the **MAP** for this new product." Then conclude with, "Now let's take one last look at our **MAP**." This is especially effective for ending your speech. Giving an audience memory joggers and reviewing your key points before you leave the platform prompts the audience to purposeful action—and they will remember you as a purposeful speaker!

Rule 5: Use an Authoritative Voice. This point is so obvious it can be easily overlooked: Your audience must be able to *hear* you. A resonant, authoritative voice is essential for effective speaking. If your voice is thin, you can teach yourself to project.

I had been a public speaker for twenty years when I was hired by a utility company to take part in its economic education program. After my first appearance, my boss came to me in shock. "You have a good and interesting conversational voice," he said, "but it falls flat in an auditorium." But then he quickly added, "Don't worry, I'll show you how to correct it." And he did.

He had me say the five vowels into a tape recorder, and then he stopped the recorder. Then he had me take a deep, diaphragmatic breath and say "maining" with enough resonance to make my nose vibrate. I went on with the other vowel sounds, carefully taking a deep breath before each word: "meaning, mining, moaning, mooning." Then I did the same exercise with shorter words, emphasizing resonance each time: "main, mean, mine, moan, moon." Finally, I practiced, "may, me, my, mow, moo." Then we turned on the recorder again and I repeated the five vowels. When we played the new set back to back with my first pronunciation test, the difference was like night and day.

Repeating vowels with a resonant voice gives you a pattern for practice in increasing depth and authority. Try this, and prove its effectiveness for yourself!

Rule 6: Speak Clearly. This goes hand in hand with rule 5. Your audience must be able to hear what you say, *and* they must be able to understand you. Remember the rules you learned in third grade: Speak clearly; don't mumble; don't swallow syllables; don't fade away at the ends of sentences.

To demonstrate that clarity and loudness are not the same thing, try this exercise. Say a few words in a whisper; imagine that you are trying to make someone six feet away from you understand. Then bring in someone, and whisper from varying distances. This is an excellent way to practice articulation.

PRACTICE MAKES PERFECT

Above all, proper preparation and practice are essential to effective speaking. Whether you are speaking to a group of ten for ten minutes or a standing-room-only crowd for a half-day seminar, you have to:

• Outline the major points of your speech.
• Memorize the key points, using your blueprint of choice.
• Practice the speech over and over again with a tape recorder.

The more often you speak before an audience, the easier the process becomes. One excellent source for practice and training is the Toastmasters Club. Your YWCA, YMCA, or chamber of commerce can locate one for you; or check the white pages of your telephone directory. Many clubs in large corporations meet at lunchtime. Join one and you'll have the chance to speak or evaluate other speakers' capabilities. Not only will you be able to practice the basic elements and fine points of public speaking, you'll acquire the polish that distinguishes the "just-OK" speaker from the "speaker-in-demand."

Sincerity is more powerful than genius or talent. If you believe strongly in what you want to say, organize your presentation, and remember your points, sincerity will carry the day for you.

VERBATIM MEMORY

There usually is a point in a speech where a quotation or an affirmation can produce a powerful effect. On those occasions, you must remember the text word for word. Many top speakers have told me that lines from "Invictus" by William Henley are among the most powerful for inspirational speakers. Let's look at the first verse and see how to memorize it:

> *Out of the night that covers me,*
> *Black as the pit from pole to pole*
> *I thank whatever gods may be*
> *For my unconquerable soul.*

Most of us start memorizing by reading the text over and over and then trying to recite it. Usually we get stuck where there is a break in the meaning, where a new thought is introduced. If, however, we could bridge that gap with a word from a prompter, we could continue. You can build your own prompters by using Memory Blueprint 7 (The Chain).

In this case, take the last two words of the first line—"covers me"—and add them to the first word of the second line—"black"—to create the phrase "covers me black." You have just created a chain tying the first and second lines together. To remember the next line, you might think of "the Pole I thank," and so on. This takes practice and repetition, but if you build your own bridges of meaning—no matter how illogical—to link the lines, you'll progress steadily through a piece of poetry or prose.

Memory Blueprint 2 (Spaces Around Your Body) is another good way to memorize passages. For example, I find that quotations from the Bible are effective additions to speeches. Once I wanted to remember the six verses in the Twenty-Third Psalm. I chose a key word from each verse and pictured it in its place: "Shepherd" was to my left, "green pastures" in front of me, "soul" to my right, "shadow" behind me, "table" under my feet, and "goodness" on my head.

Achieving verbatim memory is not easy. It takes a lot of repetition to implant the material thoroughly. But once there, you'll find that it frees you to think about conveying the meaning of the word you are speaking rather than worrying about the next word.

BUILDING A VITAL VOCABULARY

Public speaking requires an active and powerful vocabulary. Memory can help you. A sure-fire way to pick up new words and make them stick is to find meaning in their sound or appearance. This is called finding a memory bridge.

For example, the first time I heard the word "hubris," I looked it up in the dictionary for its definition, "excessive pride." Then, just as quickly, I forgot it! So when I came across it again, I had to go back to the dictionary. This time I used a memory bridge to remember it. I asked myself, "Where do the sounds 'hu' and 'bris' appear?" and decided they occurred in the name Hugh and the first syllable of "bristles." Then I said to myself, "**HUGH BRIS**tles with excessive pride." This locked the word into my memory. To remember "paradigm" (pronounced *paradime* and meaning a model), I think of making a model out of a **PAIR O' DIMES;** to remember "algorithm" (meaning program, reminding me that my friend Al Gore writes computer programs), I think of a blood-testing program that would be **ALL GORE.** Practice building memorable meanings in your highly individual way for the new words you encounter and the old words you always forget.

Let's look at a few other examples:

scintillate (to be sparkling and witty): If you **SIN TILL LATE,** you may not be sparkling and witty.

soporific (inducing or bringing on sleep): Remember Sam? He was **SO POOR** a speaker he put us to sleep!

tangent (to touch slightly or gently): At the tanning center, they **TAN GENT**ly with a touch of ultraviolet rays.

ENHANCING YOUR SPELLING ABILITY

There are times when you will be distributing copies of your remarks to your audience. Misspelled words will negatively affect your overall presentation, and may reflect unfavorably on your other abilities.

How's your spelling? Look carefully at the following words taken from a list of the 100 words most frequently misspelled in business (Figure 1). They represent four types of spelling errors. In which column is the spelling correct?

One Wrong Letter Inserted

existance	*existence*
exorbitent	*exorbitant*
concensus	*consensus*
entercede	*intercede*
seperate	*separate*

Figure 1. A checklist for your spelling skill.

Here is a list of 100 business words most frequently misspelled; check your spelling ability.

accessible	*exhilarate*
accommodate	*existence*
accrued	*exorbitant*
acquitted	*extension*
across	
allege	*grammar*
allotted	
all right	*harass*
apparel	*height*
athletics	*hyprocrisy*
audible	
auxiliary	*illegible*
	incredible
benefited	*inoculate*
besiege	*intercede*
bookkeeper	*irresistible*
calendar	*laboratory*
Cincinnati	*legitimate*
cite (quotation)	*license*
collateral	*loneliness*
concession	
consensus	*mail chute*
counterfeit	*maintenance*
	management
develop	*mileage*
dictionary	*misspell*
disappear	*momentous*
disappoint	*mucilage*
discipline	
dissatisfied	*Niagara*
dissimilar	*ninth*
	noticeable
eligible	
embarrass	*occasion*
enervate	*occurred*
equipped	*occurrence*
especially	*ofttimes*

omission	seize
omitted	sentinel
optimistic	separate
	sergeant
pamphlet	serviceable
penitentiary	site (a place)
personnel	strictly
persuade	superintendent
precede	supersede
preferring	
prejudice	tragedy
principal (primary)	transient
procedure	typing
profession	
pronunciation	
	unmanageable
questionnaire	
	welfare
recommend	whose
referring	
repetition	
restaurant	yield

Adding an Extra Letter

develope	develop
atheletic	athletic
innoculate	inoculate
wellfare	welfare
proffession	profession

Forgetting a Double Letter

aparel	apparel
bookeeper	bookkeeper
embarass	embarrass
iresistible	irresistible
questionaire	questionnaire

Omitting a Silent Letter

auxilary	auxiliary
exilarate	exhilarate
milage	mileage

Visualization can keep you out of spelling trouble. Basically the problem with spelling boils down to the fact that most of us spell by ear. In the electronic age, more of what we learn comes through sound than through the printed page, so we spell words as they sound rather than as they look. To remedy this, you can reinforce your spelling memory by putting your vision to work. Look at the four problem areas again.

1. *One wrong letter inserted.* Example: "existance" instead of "existence." Remedy: Write the word five times but with the second *e* capitalized, like this: "existEnce, existEnce, existEnce, existEnce, existEnce." You are visualizing with a little flip of the imagination to make the point more penetrating. Look over the list in Figure 1 and see if any of your misspellings fell into this first group. If so, why not correct them now before going on to the next common error?

2. *Adding an extra letter.* Example: "atheletic" instead of "athletic." Remedy: Write the word five times *incorrectly*, but insert a big cross through that extra *e*, like this: "athₑletic, athₑletic, athₑletic, athₑletic, athₑletic." You've created a visual warning just like a skull and crossbones on a bottle of poison.

3. *Forgetting a double letter.* Example: "embarass" instead of "embarrass." Remedy: Write it correctly five times. Make big letters and underscore them, like this: "emba**RR**ass, emba**RR**ass, emba**RR**ass, emba**RR**ass, emba**RR**ass."

4. *Forgetting a silent letter.* Example: "milage" instead of "mileage." Remedy: Capitalize the silent letter and bond it to the one that makes the sound, like this: "milEage, milEage, milEage, milEage, milEage."

In addition to doing these visualizing exercises, you can also create memory pictures to remind you of the correct spellings. For instance, put a "pie" in the word "piece" and picture eating a **PIE**ce of pie. Rhyming also works. You no doubt remember this schoolchildren's rhyme:

> *I* before e except after c
> Or when sounded like a
> As in "ne*i*ghbor" and "we*i*gh."

11

Remembering Numbers and Data

The man who tells me he can't remember figures tells me he can't remember the essential parts of his business and is operating on quicksand!

That statement was made by Ben Love, chief executive officer of Texas Commerce Bancshares, in an article in *Fortune* Magazine in 1978.[1] Ten years later, Mr. Love, still CEO, told me that his bank was the only large bank in Texas that had not required outside capital to survive the disastrous period when hundreds of banks sank into economic quicksand.

Knowledge of figures does imply a detailed knowledge of any subject. The person who can remember sales and marketing data, regulation numbers, and other business figures makes an unforgettable impression.

CHOOSING FROM THREE TECHNIQUES FOR REMEMBERING NUMBERS

Sometimes I meet people who insist they can't remember numbers. "My mind just doesn't work that way," they say. "I can remember anything else, but not numbers." If that sounds like you, you *can* learn to develop your memory for numbers. In fact, you can choose three ways to remember numbers:

1. You can group them;
2. You can associate them with other numbers that already have some meaning for you; or

3. You can create meaningful words or mental graphics representing numbers and read them from your memory screen.

Grouping Saves Groping. Numbers are easier to remember if you group them. The telephone company divides numbers into groups of three and four digits. Your Social Security number is composed of three groups of three, two, and four digits. That's much easier to remember than nine unbroken numbers. Think of the number $121,052,472 as 121-052-472; in the same way, 59930977 can be grouped as 59-93-09-77.

Associations Add Impact. *Controlled association* permits you to take a number that has some meaning for you—1492, 1776, or the year of your birth—and use that meaning to remember the number in a different context.

You can also use a time of day. Need to remember your lunch date with Mrs. King at 12:15? Picture the king and his courtiers sitting down for lunch at 12:15 to sign the Magna Carta in the year 1215.

You can also add meaning by turning a number into a price. Suppose your doctor's phone number is 315-8973. Imagine calling the doctor at 3:15 A.M and him charging you $89.73 for telling you to take two aspirin!

Exaggeration also helps. Suppose someone says, "I'm on the eighteenth floor at 36 Columbia Avenue." You quickly imagine painting "1836" or "3618" in big figures on the office building.

Pictures Make Numbers Graphic. Creating mental graphics or words representing numbers works well for some people. A few years ago I met a man who was studying for an exam for police chief. He was having trouble remembering the chapter and section of the law for certain offenses. He told me, as an example, that Section 314 applied to rude and disorderly conduct. I asked him if he knew anyone who lived at number 314 on any street, and he did. I suggested that he picture himself arresting that person for the offense. He used this technique for many other laws, and not only did he become chief, he set records for training his officers quickly.

Converting numbers to words is an especially easy way to remember telephone numbers. Just create words from the letters on the dial. Businesses often advertise their phone number in the form of a word, particularly if that word ties into their product. A carpet cleaning company may advertise in the local Yellow Pages: "Just dial CARPETS—227-7387." To illustrate its phone number, one direct-mail house created a Chinese girl, "MAI LING," and ran a picture of her in its ads. You can use the same technique to remember numbers that you call frequently. Since each dial number has three letters to choose from, you can almost always find some combination that creates a memorable word or phrase.

ALL-PURPOSE MEMORY CODE FOR NUMBERS

A simple memory code was popularized in 1807 by memory expert Gregor Von Feinagle, from whom we also get the term "finagle." The code is a way to make words out of numbers, and can be used for any type of information.

You can learn the code in less than an hour. If you follow my directions exactly and do the exercises step by step, you won't have to make an effort to remember anything. In spite of that you will find yourself remembering numbers and chuckling to yourself all the way to the memory bank.

Von Feinagle's code makes it possible to make a word out of any number by substituting the sounds of certain consonants for digits and then using the vowels (*a, e, i, o, u*) and the letters *w*, *h*, and *y* as memory handles or wild cards to create words. (You can remember this by thinking, **"WHY** are the vowels wild?")

For example, the digit "1" has the sound of *t*. So a word for the number "11" is any word with two *t* sounds separated by a vowel. It could be TaT, ToT, or TuT. The sounds are what count; the vowels have no numerical value.

Here are the codes for the digits 0 through 5.

0 = **S** or **Z**
1 = **T**
2 = **N**
3 = **M**
4 = **R**
5 = **L**

The following two-word phrases represent the last four digits of phone numbers. The consonant sounds are capitalized; wild cards or memory handles are in small letters. Using the guide, fill in the number opposite the words. Don't try to remember anything; just decode the words.

TiNy ToT.   _____

TiNy NuN.   _____

NoSy MaMa.   _____

NoSy MaN.   _____

MiTey RaT.   _____

Now check to see if you had the following numbers: 1211, 1222, 2033, 2032, and 3141.

If you missed any, recheck the number-letter guide, correct you mistakes, and continue.

RaRe MaN.   _____

ReaR SeaT.   _____

ReaL LaTe.   _____

LaTe MaLe.   _____

MeaN LiaR.   _____

I'm sure you had them all correct. Here are the answers: 4432, 4401, 4551, 5135, 3254.

Now for the second half of the code:

6 = J or **SH**
7 = K, hard c, or **CK**
8 = F
9 = P

You'll note that 6 and 7 have alternate letters; this increases the range of possible words. Thus the number 61 could be either JeT or <u>SH</u>oT. And 77 could be CooKie, Ki<u>CK</u>, CoCoa, or KooK—whichever works best in the particular situation. The sound of the consonant is the important part; the underline bonding of two letters is to emphasize that they make just one sound. The codes for 8 and 9 are straightforward; 81 could be FaT, 91 could be PoT.

Here is the entire number code, arranged *alphabetically:*

  C = 7 (hard *c*, like *k*)
<u>CK</u> = 7
  F = 8
  J = 6
  K = 7
  L = 5
 M = 3
 N = 2
  P = 9
  R = 4
  S = 0
<u>SH</u> = 6
  T = 1
  Z = 0

Using all nine digits, decode the following words. Refer to the alphabetical guide if you need to.

JeT MaiL	6 1 3 5	MiTey LouSe	_____
SHooT JeT	6 1 6 1	LaP JaM	_____
TaKe CaKe	_____	Ki<u>CK</u> JiM	_____
FaT CooKie	_____	CaN JaM	_____
FaT PoP	_____	Pu<u>SH</u> CooKie	_____

Here are the answers:

  6135   3150
  6161   5963
  1777   7763

8177　　7263
8199　　9677

There you have the entire code. Bear in mind it is the *sound* of the consonant that counts. When there are two of the *same* consonants together as in **Co**F**f**ee, they represent one sound. **Co**F**f**ee has only one *f* sound and represents 78, not 788.

THE FUN WAY TO LEARN THE CODE

Remember I promised that you could learn the code in less than an hour? You just did it! But unless you put it to use, the code will fade from your mind. For practice, I have developed a fun-filled way to use the code, making funny words from the phone numbers of your friends. Now that you've worked through the learning exercises, you're ready to start.

First jot down the last four digits of a telephone number you already know—for example, 1282. Then follow these five easy steps:

1. Divide your number into two pairs, like this: 12-82.
2. Refer to the list of funny phrases for phone numbers in Figure 2. Notice that the consonant sounds are capitalized and that the words in the first column sometimes modify those in the second. That's because a phrase is easier to remember than two unrelated words.
3. Locate the first pair—in my case, 12.
4. Write the first word opposite that pair—**TiNy**.
5. Locate the next pair of numbers—82—and write down the *second* word opposite that pair—**FaN**. Write the two words side by side—**TiNy FaN**.

You have now converted numbers into words. If you find it makes a funny, interesting, saucy combination, it will be easy for you to remember the code. You will also be able to create additional words that may be more significant or memorable. For instance, besides **TiNy**, 12 also could be **TiN**, **ToN**, **ToNey**, or **TuNa**. The pair 82 could be **FuN**, **FuNny**, or **FiNe**. Now take

Figure 2. Funny phrases for phone numbers.

To memorize the last four digits of any phone number, first split the number into two pairs. Look up the first pair and jot down the first word next to it; then look up the second pair and note the second word opposite it. Together they'll form a memorable phrase. Example: 1282 (12-82) is TiNy FaN.

The consonants carry the code; they are capitalized. The lower-case vowels are "wild cards" that enable you to form words. Double capitals—<u>CK</u> and <u>SH</u>—are bonded together as one sound. In a few cases, phonetic spellings are used. Example: 28 is NiFe ("knife").

00	SeiZe	SiZe	33	MuM	MaMa
01	SweeT	SeaT	34	MoRe	MaRe
02	SuNny	SiN	35	MaLe	MiLe
03	SeeM	SuM	36	Mu<u>SH</u>y	Ma<u>SH</u>
04	SoRe	SiR	37	MaKe	MiKe
05	SiLly	SaLe	38	MiFf	MuFf
06	Swi<u>SH</u>	Sa<u>SH</u>	39	MoPey	MoP
07	Si<u>CK</u>	Sa<u>CK</u>	40	RoSy	RoSe
08	SaFe	SoFa	41	RoT	RaT
09	SoaPy	SouP	42	RuiN	RaiN
10	TieS	ToeS	43	RuMmy	RooM
11	TiTe	ToT	44	RaRe	ReaR
12	TiNy	TiN	45	ReaL	RaiL
13	TuMmy	TeaM	46	Ra<u>SH</u>	Ru<u>SH</u>
14	TeaR	TaR	47	Ro<u>CK</u>y	Ro<u>CK</u>
15	TaLl	TaLe	48	RuFf	RooF
16	Ti<u>SH</u>ue	Ta<u>SH</u>a	49	RiP	RoPe
17	Ta<u>CK</u>y	Ti<u>CK</u>	50	LooSe	LouSe
18	TuFf	TaFfy	51	LaTe	LiTe
19	ToP	TaPe	52	LeaN	LiNe
20	NoSy	NooSe	53	LaMe	LiMe
21	NeaT	NeT	54	LeeRy	LiaR
22	NoNe	NooN	55	LiLy	LuLu
23	NaMe	NeMo	56	Lu<u>SH</u>	La<u>SH</u>
24	NeaR	NeRo	57	Lu<u>CK</u>y	Lo<u>CK</u>
25	NaiL	NiLe	58	LiFe	LeaF
26	Na<u>SH</u>	No<u>SH</u>	59	LiPpy	LaP
27	Ni<u>CK</u>	Ne<u>CK</u>	60	JaZzy	JaZz
28	NiFe	NuFf	61	JoT	JeT
29	NiP	NaP	62	JohNny	JohN
30	MeSsy	Moose	63	JiMmy	JaM
31	MiTey	MaT	64	JeeR	JaR
32	MeaN	Moon	65	JeweL	JaiL

(continued)

Figure 2 *(continued)*

66	JuDGe	JuDGe*	83	FoaMy	FaMe
67	JaCK	JaCK	84	FaiR	FuR
68	JiFfy	JeFf	85	FLy	FoiL
69	JiP	JeeP	86	FiSHy	FiSH
70	CoZy	CaSe	87	FaKe	FaKe
71	CuTe	CaT	88	FiFe	FiFe
72	CaNny	CaN	89	FoP	FaP
73	CoMe	CoMb	90	PaSs	PieS
74	CaRry	CaR	91	PaT	PoT
75	CooL	CoaL	92	PuNy	PaN
76	CaSH	CaSH	93	PuMa	PoeM
77	CooK	CaKe	94	PuRe	PaiR
78	CuFf	CoFfee	95	PaLe	PaiL
79	CoPy	CuP	96	PuSH	PuSH
80	FuSsy	FuSe	97	PiCKy	PaCK
81	FaT	FooT	98	PuFfy	PuFf
82	FiNe	FaN	99	PuPpy	PoP

*__DG__ sounds like *J*.

a few numbers you already know and see what interesting pairs of words you can find for the last four digits of each number. If you discover some memorable words, the new code will be locked into your mind because of the firm association with numbers and digits you already know.

I started with the last four digits because that's where people usually have trouble. The first three digits seem easier for most of us to remember, partly because each community has a limited number of prefixes, and over time we tend to learn them and perhaps even associate them with certain parts of town. But when you're learning new ones, simply use the same principles: Make up a word or phrase using the three consonant codes. Examples: 275 is NiCKeL and 558 is Low LiFe. See Figure 4, The Number Dictionary, for others. It gives the word equivalents for every three-digit number from 000 to 999. Take a minute now to practice looking up a few numbers.

Use the same procedure to remember area codes, making up words from the consonant sounds and filling in with vowels. To get you started, refer to Figure 3, Words for Remembering Telephone Area Codes. To further lock the code into your memory, try to come up with words that have an association for you. For

Figure 3. Words for remembering area codes.

Digits from 0 to 9 are assigned consonant codes. Using the sounds of the consonants, filled in with vowels to make words, you can create words and phrases to remember area codes. The codes listed here (some are spelled phonetically) are merely examples; the possibilities are endless.

To further lock the code into your memory, think of the telephone area codes you already know. Locate them on the list and see what words fit.

201	NeST	401	RuST
202	iNSaNe	402	RaiSiN
203	No SaM	403	ReSuMe
204	No SiR	404	RiSeR
205	NaSaL	405	ReSaLe
206	NoSy Joe	406	RoSe SHow
207	New SoCK	407	RiSK
208	uNSaFe	408	RiSe oFf
209	No SoaP	412	RiTe oN
212	aNTeNna	413	RiTe Me
213	aNaToMy	414	RoTaRy
214	NoT heRe	415	RaTtLe
215	NeTtLe	416	RiTe SHoe
216	NiTe SHow	417	ReTaKe
217	aNTiC	418	RaTiFy
218	NiTe oFf	419	RiTe uP
219	No ToP		
301	MaST	501	LoST
302	MaSoN	502	LeSsoN
303	MuSeuM	503	LoSe Me
304	MiSeR	504	LoSeR
305	MiSsiLe	505	LooSe Law
306	MiSs Joe	506	LooSe SHoe
307	MaSK	507	aLaSKa
308	My SaFe	508	aLl SaFe
309	haM SouP	509	LiSP
312	MiTteN	512	LaTiN
313	My TeaM	513	LeT Me
314	MuTteR	514	LeTteR
315	MeTaL	515	LiTtLe
316	MeaT haSH	516	LaTe SHow
317	MeaT hooK	517	LiTe Key
318	MoTiF	518	LiTe oFf
319	MeaT Pie	519	LeT uP

(continued)

Figure 3 *(continued)*

601	JuST	801	FaST
602	JaSoN	802	Few SiN
603	JoySoMe	803	FuSsy Ma
604	Joe'S haiR	804	FuSseR
605	Joe'S oiL	805	FuSe oiL
606	Joe'S Jaw	806	FuSe SHow
607	Joy SaCK	807	FiSK
608	JoSeF	808	Few SaFe
609	Joe'S Pa	812	FaTteN
612	JiTNey	813	FaTiMa
613	JeT 'eM	814	FaTteR
614	JeTter	815	FaTaL
615	JeT hoLe	816	FaT Jaw
616	JeT SHow	817	Few TaKe
617	Joe TooK	818	FiTe oFf
618	JeT oFf	819	FaT Pay
619	Jet uP		
		901	PoST
701	CaST	902	PoiSoN
702	CaSiNo	904	PaSseR
703	KiSs Me	906	PayS Joe
704	KisSeR	907	PaSs Key
705	KiSs Lee	912	PuT oN
707	CaSK	913	PaT Me
709	KiSs Pa	914	PoTteR
712	CoTtoN	915	PoT hoLe
713	CuT Me	916	PoT aSH
714	CuTteR	918	PuT oFf
715	CaTtLe	919	PoT Pie
716	CuTe SHow		
717	CuT Key		

instance, 202 (Washington, D.C.) could be iNSaNe. Nevada's code, 702, translates into **CaSiNo**, and Hollywood's 213 provides aNaToMy.

Remember to listen to consonant sounds only. You could use any word with similar sounds. The code 402, for example, could be **ReaSoN**, **RiSe oN**, or **ouR SiN**; 302 could be **My SoN** or **My SiN**; 914 could be **PuTteR** or **PuT heRe**. The illustrations are endless, but the principle is the same.

OTHER APPLICATIONS FOR THE CODE

Once you develop a ready and reliable memory for the code, you can use it in many ways in your personal and professional life.

Most numbers are broken down by threes and separated by commas and, in the case of money amounts, a decimal point followed by a two-digit number. For example, let's take the number I used earlier: $121,052,472. Using the dictionary in Figure 4 for 121 I find **TNT;** for 052 I get **SaLooN;** and for 472, there is **RaCcooN.** Now, to remember the full number, imagine yourself using **TNT** to blow up the **SaLooN** and in the process, scaring the daylights out of the **RaCcooN.**

(text continues on page 132)

Figure 4.   The number dictionary.

000–099

000	Say SuSie	028	SNiFf
001	hiS SeaT	029	SNiP
002	SeaSoN	030	SeeMs
003	SeSaMe	031	SuMmiT
004	SeeS heR	032	See Me oN
005	SeeS aLl	033	See MaMa
006	SeeS SHow	034	SMeaR
007	Sea SiCK	035	SMiLe
008	SeeS oFf	036	SMaSH
009	SeeS Pay	037	SMaCK
010	STayS	038	See Me oFf
011	STaTe	039	SuM uP
012	STaiN	040	SeaRS
013	STeaM	041	SoRT
014	STaR	042	SiReN
015	STiLl	043	SeRuM
016	STaSH	044	See ReaR
017	STiCK	045	SeRiaL
018	STuFf	046	SoRe Jaw
019	SToP	047	See RoCK
020	SiNS	048	SeRF
021	SNooTy	049	SyRuP
022	SiNe oN	050	SeLlS
023	hiS NaMe	051	SaLuTe
024	SNeeR	052	SaLooN
025	See NeLlie	053	SLaM
026	SiN SHow	054	SaiLoR
027	SNaKe	055	See LiLy

(continued)

Figure 4 *(continued)*

056	SLaSH	078	SKiFf
057	SLiCK	079	SCooP
058	Sea LiFe	080	SaFeS
059	SLaP	081	SoFT
060	See SHoeS	082	See FaNny
061	Say SHooT	083	Sea FoaM
062	See JohN	084	SuFfeR
063	See SHiMmy	085	iS FuLl
064	Sea SHoRe	086	Sea FiSH
065	Sea SHeLl	087	See FaKe
066	See JuDGe*	088	SaFe Fee
067	Say JaCK	089	SaFe Pay
068	See SHeaf	090	SPieS
069	See SHiP	091	SpoT
070	SKieS	092	SpiN
071	SCooT	093	SPaM
072	SCaN	094	SPeaR
073	SKiM	095	SPiLl
074	SCoRe	096	SoaP SHow
075	SLiLl	097	SPeaK
076	See CaSH	098	See PuFfy
077	Sea CooK	099	SoaP uP

100–199

100	ThiS iS	121	TNT
101	TeST	122	Tie oNe oN
102	TieS iN	123	TiNy Meow
103	TeaSe Me	124	TuNeR
104	TeaSeR	125	TuNneL
105	TaSseL	126	TiNy SHoe
106	Tie SaSH	127	TaNK
107	TaSK	128	Tie oNe OFf
108	TieS oFf	129	TuNe uP
109	TieS uP	130	TuMS
110	TooTS	131	Tie MeeT
111	TiTe Tie	132	Tie MaN
112	TiTeN	133	TiMe Me
113	Tea TiMe	134	Tie MoRe
114	ToTeR	135	Tie MuLe
115	TiTLe	136	TeaM SHow
116	TiTe SHoe	137	ToMahawK
117	Tie TaCK	138	Tie MuFf
118	Tie iT oFf	139	TaMP
119	Tie iT uP	140	TRieS
120	TiNeS	141	TRy ouT

*DG has the sound of J.

142	TRy oN	171	TaKe ouT
143	TRiM	172	Tie CaN
144	TRy heR	173	TaKe Me
145	TRoLl	174	TiCKeR
146	TRaSH	175	TiCKLe
147	TRuCK	176	TaKe SHoe
148	TeaR oFf	177	TaKe Key
149	TRiP	178	TaKe oFf
150	ToiLS	179	TaKe uP
151	ToiLeT	180	TuFfeeS
152	TaLoN	181	TuFT
153	TeLl Me	182	TuFfeN
154	TaiLoR	183	TaFfy Ma
155	TeLl aLl	184	TuFfeR
156	TeLl SHow	185	TuFf Law
157	TaLC	186	TuFf SHoe
158	TeLl oFf	187	TuFf Key
159	TuLiP	188	TuFf Fee
160	Tie SHoeS	189	TuFf Pay
161	Tie SHeeT	190	ToPS
162	Too ShiNy	191	Tea PoT
163	To SHaMe	192	TiP oN
164	To SHoRe	193	TiP Me
165	Tie SHawL	194	TiPpeR
166	Tie JuDGe*	195	TiPpLe
167	Tie SHaCK	196	Tie uP SHoe
168	Tie SHeaF	197	Tie PaCK
169	Tie SHoP	198	TiP oFf
170	TaKeS	199	TiP uP

200–299

200	NoSeS	213	No TiMe
201	NeST	214	NoT heRe
202	No SiN	215	NeTtLe
203	No SaM	216	NeaT SHow
204	No SiR	217	New TaCK
205	No SaLe	218	NoTiFy
206	New SaSH	219	No ToP
207	New SoCK	220	NuNS
208	uNSaFe	221	New NoTe
209	No SoaP	222	No No No
210	NuTS	223	No NaMe
211	NoT iT	224	Now NeaR
212	NoT iN	225	New NaiL

*DG has the sound of J.

(continued)

Figure 4 *(continued)*

226	No New SHoe	263	No SHaMe
227	No iNK	264	No SHeRry
228	New eNuF	265	New SHawL
229	No NiP	266	New JuDGe*
230	NaMeS	267	No SHaCK
231	New MaTe	268	New SHeaF
232	New MooN	269	New SHiP
233	New MuMu	270	NeCKS
234	Now MaRy	271	uNCuT
235	No MeaL	272	New CaNe
236	No MaSH	273	NiCK Me
237	No MiKe	274	No CaR
238	NaMe oF	275	NiCKeL
239	New MoP	276	No CaSH
240	NuRSe	277	New CaKe
241	NoRTh	278	NoCK oFf
242	No RaiN	279	New CoP
243	No RooM	280	No FeeS
244	NeaReR	281	No FeeT
245	No RaiL	282	No FuN
246	No RuSH	283	No FoaM
247	New yoRK	284	No FiRe
248	New RooF	285	New FoiL
249	New RoPe	286	No FiSH
250	NaiLS	287	No FaKe
251	New LiTe	288	New FiFe
252	NyLoN	289	NiFe Pie
253	New LoaM	290	NiPS
254	NaiLeR	291	New PoT
255	New LiLy	292	NiPpoN
256	NaiL SHoe	293	New PoeM
257	No LuCK	294	NiPpeR
258	New LiFe	295	NiPpLe
259	NaiL uP	296	No PuSH
260	New SHoeS	297	No PiCK
261	New JeT	298	NiP oFf
262	No SHiNe	299	New PuPpy

300–399

300	MiSseS	306	My SaSH
301	MoST	307	MaSK
302	MaSoN	308	My SaFe
303	MiSs Me	309	My SoaP
304	MiSeR	310	MiTtS
305	MiSsiLe	311	My ToT

*DG has the sound of J.

312	MiTteN	356	MaiL SHoe
313	My TeaM	357	MiLK
314	MoTheR	358	My LiFe
315	MeTaL	359	My LaP
316	MiTey SHow	360	My SHoeS
317	My TaCK	361	My SHeeT
318	My TaFfy	362	My SHiNe
319	My ToP	363	My SHaMe
320	MiNeS	364	MaSHeR
321	MiNuTe	365	My SHawL
322	MiNioN	366	My JuDGe*
323	My NaMe	367	My SHaCK
324	MiNoR	368	My SHeaF
325	MaNuaL	369	MaSH uP
326	My New SHoe	370	MaKeS
327	MiNK	371	MaKe ouT
328	My NiFe	372	My CaNe
329	MoNey uP	373	MaKe Me
330	MuMS	374	MoCKeR
331	MaMmoTh	375	Me CooL
332	My MaN	376	My CaSH
333	My My My	377	My CaKe
334	MuMmeR	378	My CoFfee
335	MaMmaL	379	MaKe uP
336	My MaSH	380	MuFfS
337	MiMiC	381	My FeeT
338	My MuFf	382	My FaNny
339	My MaP	383	My FaMe
340	MaRS	384	My FiRe
341	MeRiT	385	MuFfLe
342	MaRiNe	386	My FiSH
343	MiRiaM	387	Me FaKe
344	MiRroR	388	My FiFe
345	MuRaL	389	MuFf uP
346	My RuSH	390	MaPS
347	MaRK	391	MoPpeT
348	My RooF	392	My PoNy
349	My RoPe	393	My PoeM
350	MaiLS	394	MoP heR
351	MaLT	395	MaPLe
352	MiLlioN	396	Me PuSH
353	MaiL Me	397	My PaCK
354	MaiLeR	398	MoP oFf
355	MoLehiLl	399	MoP uP

*DG has the sound of J.

(continued)

Figure 4   *(continued)*

400–499

400	RaiSeS	447	ReaR Key
401	RuSTy	448	ReRooF
402	ReaSoN	449	RaRe Pay
403	ReSuMe	450	RoLlS
404	RaiSe heR	451	RoLl iT
405	RaiSe heLl	452	ReLiNe
406	RaiSe SHoe	453	ReaLM
407	RiSK	454	RoLleR
408	ouR SoFa	455	RoyaL Law
409	RaSP	456	ReLiSH
410	RaTS	457	ReLoCK
411	RiTe iT	458	ReLieF
412	RiTe oN	459	RoLl uP
413	RiTe Me	460	RuSHeS
414	RoTaRy	461	RuSH iT
415	RaTtLe	462	RuSHiaN
416	RiTe SHoe	463	RuSH Me
417	RiTe Key	464	RuSH heR
418	RiTe oFf	465	RuSH heLl
419	RiTe uP	466	RuSH SHow
420	RuiNS	467	RuSH Key
421	ReNT	468	RuSH oFf
422	ReuNioN	469	RuSH uP
423	ReNaMe	470	RoCKS
424	RuNneR	471	RoCKeT
425	RuN heLl	472	RaCcooN
426	RuiN SHoe	473	RoCK 'eM
427	RiNK	474	RoCKeR
428	RuN oFf	475	ReCaLl
429	RuN uP	476	ReCaSH
430	ReaMS	477	ReCooK
431	ReMiT	478	RaKe oFf
432	ReMaiN	479	RaCK uP
433	ouR MaMa	480	ReFuSe
434	ReaMeR	481	RaFT
435	ReMaiL	482	ReFiNe
436	RuM SHow	483	RuFf 'eM
437	ReMaKe	484	RooFeR
438	RuM Fee	485	RiFLe
439	RaMP	486	RuFf SHoe
440	RoaRS	487	RuFf Key
441	ReRiTe	488	RuFf Fee
442	ReRuN	489	RuFf uP
443	ReaRM	490	RiPS
444	Rah Rah Rah	491	RiP iT
445	RuRaL	492	RiP oN
446	RaRe SHow	493	RiP 'eM

494	RiPpeR	497	RePaCK
495	RiPpLe	498	RiP oFf
496	RoPe SHow	499	RiP uP

500–599

500	LoSeS	537	Low MiKe
501	LaST	538	Low MuFF
502	LeSsoN	539	LiMP
503	LoSe Me	540	LuReS
504	LoSeR	541	LaRiaT
505	LoSe aLl	542	LoRraiNe
506	LooSe SHoe	543	aLaRM
507	aLaSKa	544	Low ReaR
508	Lie SoFa	545	LauReL
509	LiSP	546	LoweR SHoe
510	LoTS	547	LuRK
511	LeT iT	548	Low RooF
512	LeT iN	549	LaRruP
513	LeT Me	550	LuLlS
514	LeTteR	551	LiLT
515	LiTtLe	552	Lie Low oN
516	LaTe SHow	553	Low LiMey
517	LaTe Key	554	Low LiaR
518	LaTe Fee	555	La La La
519	LiTe uP	556	LiLy SHow
520	LiNeS	557	LiLaC
521	LeNT	558	Low LiFe
522	LiNeN	559	Low LiP
523	LoaN Me	560	Low SHoeS
524	LiNeR	561	Low SHoT
525	LoaN aLl	562	LaSH oN
526	LoaN SHoe	563	LaSH Me
527	LiNK	564	LaSH heR
528	LoaN Fee	565	Low SHawL
529	LiNe uP	566	Low JuDGe*
530	LooMS	567	Low SHaCK
531	LiMiT	568	LuSH Fee
532	LeMoN	569	Low SHoP
533	Low MuMu	570	LeaKS
534	Lay MoRe	571	LoCK ouT
535	Low MeaL	572	LoCK iN
536	LiMey SHow	573	LooK Ma

*DG has the sound of J.

(continued)

Figure 4 *(continued)*

574	LoCKeR	587	Low FaKe
575	LoCaL	588	LeaF oFf
576	LiKe SHow	589	LiFe Pay
577	LoCK Key	590	LeaPS
578	LooK oFf	591	Low PoT
579	LoCK uP	592	LeaP oN
580	LiFe'S	593	LeaP Ma
581	LiFT	594	LePeR
582	Low FuN	595	LaPeL
583	Low FoaM	596	Low PuSH
584	LoaFeR	597	i'Ll PiCK
585	Lie FaiL	598	LeaP oFf
586	Low FiSH	599	LeaP uP

600–699

600	SHe SayS	633	SHow MaMa
601	SHe'S iT	634	SHow MoRe
602	SHe'S iN	635	SHow Me aLl
603	SHow SoMe	636	SHaM SHow
604	SHowS heR	637	SHow MiKe
605	SHoe SaLe	638	SHow Me oFf
606	SHow SaSH	639	SHow MaP
607	SHoe SaCK	640	SHeaRS
608	SHow SoFa	641	SHoRT
609	SHoe SoaP	642	SHaRe oNe
610	SHooTS	643	SHow RooM
611	SHooT iT	644	SHeaReR
612	SHuT iN	645	SHRiLl
613	SHooT Me	646	SHaRe SHoe
614	SHaTteR	647	SHaRK
615	SHuTtLe	648	SHeRiFf
616	SHeeT SHow	649	SHaRP
617	SHuT Key	650	SHoaLS
618	SHuT oFf	651	SHow LiTe
619	SHuT uP	652	SHow LiNe
620	SHiNeS	653	SHaLoM
621	SHaNTy	654	SHow LiaR
622	SHiNe oN	655	SHow LiLy
623	SHow NaMe	656	SHaLl SHe
624	SHiNeR	657	SHeLlaC
625	SHoe NaiL	658	SHeLF
626	SHiNe SHoe	659	SHow LiP
627	SHow NeCK	660	SHow SHoeS
628	SHiNe oFf	661	SHow SHeeT
629	SHiNe uP	662	SHoe SHiNe
630	SHiMmieS	663	SHow SHaMe
631	SHoe MaT	664	SHow SHaRe
632	SHow MaN	665	SHow SHiLl

666	SHow SHow SHow	683	SHow FaMe
		684	SHow FuR
667	SHow SHaCK	685	SHow FiLe
668	SHe SHow oFf	686	SHow FiSH
669	SHow SHiP	687	SHow FaKe
670	SHaKeS	688	SHow FiFe
671	SHaKe iT	689	SHow oFf Pie
672	SHaKe oN	690	SHoPS
673	ShaKe Me	691	SHiP iT
674	SHaKeR	692	SHiP iN
675	SHeKeL	693	SHiP Me
676	SHow CaSH	694	SHiPpeR
677	SHow CaKe	695	SHow PaL
678	SHaKe oFf	696	SHow PuSH
679	SHaKe uP	697	SHow PiCK
680	SHow FuSe	698	SHiP oFf
681	SHaFT	699	SHow PuPpy
682	SHow FuN		

700–799

700	KiSseS	728	CaN oF
701	CaST	729	CaNoPy
702	CaSiNo	730	CoMeS
703	KiSs Me	731	CoMeT
704	KiSseR	732	CoMe oN
705	Key SaLe	733	CoMe Ma
706	KiSs SHow	734	CoMe heRe
707	CaSK	735	CaMeL
708	KiSs oFf	736	CoMe SHow
709	KiSs Pie	737	CoMe Kay
710	CuTieS	738	CoMFy
711	CuT iT	739	CaMP
712	CoTtoN	740	CRieS
713	CuT Me	741	CRaTe
714	CuTteR	742	CRayoN
715	CaTtLe	743	CReaM
716	CuTe SHoe	744	CaReeR
717	CuTe Key	745	CRueL
718	CuT oFf	746	CRuSH
719	CuT uP	747	CRaCK
720	CaNS	748	CaRry oFf
721	CaN'T	749	CRoP
722	CaNiNe	750	CooLS
723	CoN Me	751	CooL iT
724	CaNaRy	752	CLeaN
725	CaNaL	753	CLaM
726	CaN SHe	754	CooLeR
727	CaN Kay	755	CoaL oiL

(continued)

Figure 4 *(continued)*

756	CLaSH	778	CooK oFf
757	CLiCK	779	CooK Pie
758	CLiFf	780	CuFfS
759	CLaP	781	CuFf iT
760	CaSHeS	782	CoFfiN
761	CaSH ouT	783	CuFf Me
762	CaSH iN	784	CoiFfuRe
763	CaSH 'eM	785	CoFfee Low
764	CaSHieR	786	CuFf SHoe
765	CaSH aLl	787	CoFfee Kay
766	CaSH SHow	788	CoFfee oFf
767	CaSH Key	789	CoFfee Pie
768	CaSH Fee	790	CuPS
769	CaSH Pay	791	CuP iT
770	CooKS	792	CouPoN
771	CooK ouT	793	CaP Me
772	CooK oN	794	CoPpeR
773	CooK Ma	795	CouPLe
774	CooKeR	796	CuP SHow
775	CooK aLl	797	CuP hooK
776	CaKe SHow	798	CaP oFf
777	KKK	799	CoP Pay

800–899

800	FuSeS	823	FiNe Me
801	FaST	824	FiNeR
802	FuSe iN	825	FuNneL
803	FuSsy Me	826	FuN SHow
804	FuSsieR	827	FiNK
805	FuSe hoLe	828	FuN Fee
806	FuSsy SHe	829	FuNny Pie
807	FuSe Key	830	FuMeS
808	FuSs oFf	831	Few MeeT
809	FuSs uP	832	Foe MaN
810	FaTSo	833	Few MoM
811	FaT Tie	834	FoaMieR
812	FaTteN	835	FeMaLe
813	FaTiMa	836	FaMiSH
814	FaTheR	837	Few MaKe
815	FooT hoLe	838	FoaM oFf
816	FaT SHow	839	FoaM uP
817	FaT Kay	840	FRieS
818	FaT Fee	841	FReT
819	FaT Pie	842	FeRN
820	FiNeS	843	FRoM
821	FouNT	844	FRieR
822	FiNe oN	845	FRiLl

846	FReSH	873	FaKe Me
847	FRoCK	874	FaKeR
848	FiRe oFf	875	FiCKLe
849	FiRe uP	876	FaKe SHow
850	FLieS	877	FaKe Cow
851	FloaT	878	Fake Fee
852	FiLl iN	879	Fake Pie
853	FLaMe	880	Few FuSs
854	FLieR	881	FiFTh
855	FLaiL	882	Few FuNny
856	FLeSH	883	Few FaMe
857	FLoCK	884	Few FoR
858	FLuFf	885	Few FiKe
859	FLoP	886	Few FiSH
860	FiSHeS	887	Few FaKe
861	FiSH iT	888	Fee Fie Foe
862	FiSH iN	889	Few Fee Pay
863	FiSH My	890	Few PieS
864	FiSH heRe	891	Few Pay iT
865	FiSH hoLe	892	Few Pay iN
866	FiSH SHow	893	Few Pay Me
867	FiSH hooK	894	Few Pay heR
868	FiSH oFf	895	Few PuLl
869	FiSH Pie	896	Few PuSH
870	FaKeS	897	Few PiCK
871	FaCT	898	Few Pay oFf
872	FaKe oNe	899	Few Pay uP

900–999

900	PaSseS	919	PoT Pie
901	PoST	920	PiNS
902	PoiSoN	921	PoiNT
903	Pay SoMe	922	PiN oN
904	PaSseR	923	PaNaMa
905	PayS aLl	924	Pay NeaR
906	PaSs SHow	925	PaNeL
907	PaSs Key	926	Pay No SHow
908	PayS oFf	927	PiNK
909	Pea SouP	928	Pay eNuFf
910	PaTS	929	PiN uP
911	PuT iT	930	PoeMS
912	PaT oN	931	Pay MaTe
913	PaT Me	932	Pie MaN
914	PaT heR	933	Pay MaMa
915	PoT hoLe	934	Pay MoRe
916	PoTaSH	935	PuMmeL
917	PuT Key	936	Pay My SHow
918	PuT oFf	937	Pay MiCKey

(continued)

Figure 4 *(continued)*

938	Pay Me oFf		969	PuSH uP	
939	PuMP		970	PiCKS	
940	PeeRS		971	PiCKeT	
941	PReTty		972	PeCaN	
942	PReeN		973	PiCK Me	
943	PooR Me		974	PaCKeR	
944	PRioR		975	PiCKLe	
945	Pay RoLl		976	Pay CaSH	
946	Pay RuSH		977	Pay CooKie	
947	Pay RoCKey		978	PiCK oFf	
948	PRooF		979	PiCK uP	
949	PRoP		980	PuFfS	
950	PeeLS		981	PuFf iT	
951	PLaTe		982	PuFf iN	
952	PiLe oN		983	Pay oFf Me	
953	PLuM		984	Pay FoR	
954	PLay heRe		985	PiFfLe	
955	Pay LiLy		986	Pay FiSH	
956	PLuSH		987	Pay oFf Key	
957	PLuCK		988	PuFf oFf	
958	Pay LiFe		989	PuFf uP	
959	PLoP		990	PoPS	
960	PuSHeS		991	PoP iT	
961	PuSH iT		992	PiPpiN	
962	PuSH oN		993	PoP 'eM	
963	PuSH Me		994	PiPeR	
964	PuSHeR		995	PeeP hoLe	
965	PuSH aLl		996	PeeP SHow	
966	Pay JuDGe*		997	Pay PaCK	
967	PuSH Key		998	PoP oFf	
968	PuSH oFf		999	Pay PaPa	

*DG has the sound of J.

You can use the code with all sorts of business data. These are from a bank's balance sheet:

Cash:	$ 101,054,613
Words from dictionary:	TeST, SaiLoR, SHooT Me
Time deposits:	$ 101,011,392
Words from dictionary:	TeST, STaTe, My PoNy
Loan receivables:	$ 140,786,705
Words from dictionary:	TRieS, CuFf SHoe, Key SaLe

The code can also be used to remember stock prices. If you are continually involved in the market, your interest in it and the abilities that put you in the market in the first place probably mean that you don't need this kind of assistance. But they are a good example of putting the code to use.

If you look in the financial section of the newspaper, you'll see stock prices quoted as whole numbers plus fractions; $27\frac{1}{8}$ means $27 plus one-eighth of a dollar ($12\frac{1}{2}$ cents) or $27.125. To use stock prices as numbers to practice on, consider the fraction part of a three-digit number. (Of course if the price is over $100, you'll have a four-digit number, but most stocks are under $100.) For example:

44			= ReaR
$44\frac{1}{8}$	=	441	= ReRi Te
$44\frac{1}{4}$	= $44\frac{2}{8}$ =	442	= ReRuN
$44\frac{3}{8}$	=	443	= ReaRM
$44\frac{1}{2}$	= $44\frac{4}{8}$ =	444	= Rah Rah Rah

If those happen to be the various prices of Texaco, you can associate your concept of Texaco with the pictures suggested by the words **ReaR**, **ReRite**, and so forth.

The Dow Jones Industrial Average at 2186 breaks into pairs and can be thought of as **NeT FiSH**. One pundit thinks it will hit a low of 1750, which translates into **TaKe LoSs**! However, if one of the optimists on *Wall Street Week* thinks it will go to 2920, that can be thought of as **NiP NoSe**!

Use the number dictionary (Figure 4) just as you would any dictionary or code book—when you occasionally need help remembering. If the words are more easily remembered than the numbers, the code will prove its value to you.

12

Foreign Languages For The Fast-Flying Businessperson

Many businesspeople with interests overseas spend short periods of time in different countries. They don't need to fully learn another language, but the ability to pick up and remember a few essential words can be extremely useful. This, combined with a little sign language, will ease their way in many situations where English is not spoken.

MEMORY IN ANOTHER LANGUAGE

Many phrase books show the phonetic pronunciation of foreign phrases, but I have yet to see one that explains how to remember them. Here's how you can put them in your memory bank.

1. Look at the meaning of the word and read or listen to the phonetic pronunciation. For instance, the Spanish word for "yes" is *si*, pronounced *see*.
2. Think of something in English that sounds like or looks like the foreign word. It does not have to mean the same, just sound or look the same, like *si* and *see*.
3. Make a memory bridge by connecting the meaning of the sound- or look-alike word with the meaning of the foreign word. Example: "I wanted to **SEE** if he would say *yes*." Your bridges will be highly individual because the meaning of any sound is different for different people.

Let's try a few memory bridges. As you look at the following words, think what each one sounds like to you.

Oh

Vassah

Lee

Bet

Oh is the sound of the French word for "water," *eau*. You can build a memory bridge by thinking, **"OH,** how I'd like some *water*." You have now attached the present meaning that the sound has for you to the new meaning, *water*.

Vassah, with the first *a* pronounced *ah*, is the sound of the German word for "water," *wasser*. It reminds me of Vassar College; so my memory bridge is: "The **VASSAH** girls drink only *water*."

Lee is the sound of the French word for "bed," *lit*. A memory bridge for it could be: "I want a *bed* in the **LEE** of the building." For *bett*, the German word for "bed," your memory bridge could be, "You **BET** I want a *bed*."

REMEMBERING THE ESSENTIALS

Knowing just a few essential words and phrases will go a long way toward making your travels easier and pleasanter. Six that I find particularly useful are "please," "thank you," "how much?" "too much," "sleep," and "railroad station." To help you learn and remember them, you could use Memory Blueprint 2 (Spaces Around Your Body).

Place "please" to your left, your picture for "thank you" in front of you, "how much?" to your right, "too much" behind you, "sleep" under your feet, and "railroad station" on your head. You have now set up the English words where you can think about the foreign words in order and repeatedly until you have them mastered. Of course, if some other memory blueprint works better for you, by all means use it.

Here are examples of the six words in French and German with memory bridges. Remember, the principle is that you can build a bridge between meaningful sounds even if the meaning of the words seems illogical. You can use the illogical for a logical purpose.

THE FRENCH CONNECTION

English Word	French Word	Sound	Bridge
please	*s'il vous plait*	"seal voo play"	**SEAL VIEW PLAY**

The bridge: *Please* let the **SEAL VIEW** the **PLAY**.

thank you	*merci*	"mairsee"	**MARE SEE**

The bridge: *Thank you* for letting me see the **MARE SEE**.

how much?	*combien?*	"com bee en"	**COMB BE IN**

The bridge: *How much* **COMB BE IN** a beehive?

too much	*trop*	"trow"	**THROW**

The bridge: I **THROW** *too much*

sleep	*dormir*	"door mere"	**DOOR MERE**

The bridge: I can *sleep* in a **DOOR-MERE**-tory.

railroad station	*gare*	"gar"	ci**GAR**

The bridge: I bought a big ci**GAR** at the *railroad station*.

THE GERMAN JOURNEY

English Word	German Word	Sound	Bridge
please	*bitte*	"bit-eh"	**BITTY**

The bridge: *Please* give me a little **BITTY** piece.

thank you	*danke*	"dank-eh"	**DUNKEH**

The bridge: *Thank you* for being a **DUNKER** [dankeh].

how much?	*wie viel*	"vee feel"	**VEE FEEL**

The bridge: **VEE** [we] **FEEL** we'd like to know *how much* it is.

too much	*zu viel*	"sue feel"	**SUE FEEL**

The bridge: I'll **SUE** you if I **FEEL** it's *too much*.

English Word	German Word	Sound	Bridge
sleep	*schlafen*	"schlaugh in"	**SHE'S LAUGHIN'**

The bridge: SHE'S LAUGHIN' in her *sleep*.

railroad station	*bahnhof*	"bahn off"	**BARN OF**

The bridge: It's a big **BARN OF** a *railroad station*.

Incidentally, in German, restroom doors are labeled *Damen* for women and *Herren* for men. Our word "dame" makes *Damen* easy to remember, and I think of *Herren* as "It's not **HER-EN**, it's his'n."

Here are some additional coping words:

toilet	*airport*
food	*write*
water	*spell*
bed	*draw*
eat	*right*
drink	*left*
come	*north*
go	*south*
money	*east*
bank	*west*
consul	

From this list choose the six words that you consider most essential, look up their French and German equivalents, and try the bridging technique. One last tip: Always use personal visualization. Actually picture yourself saying *merci* and *bitte*. It will make the bridge even more memorable.

LEARNING SPANISH

In this section I'll show you how to apply the principles of memory to learning Spanish. I believe you'll find it a useful guide for learning *any* foreign language.

Residents of the United States are increasingly in contact with people in Mexico, Central America, South America, and other Spanish-speaking countries. To deal effectively in these major markets, Spanish is probably the most important foreign language to learn. Some knowledge of it also is useful if you employ people whose native language is Spanish.

I taught myself Spanish, and so I think I know what will work for you on a self-instruction basis in the shortest period of time. Here are the basic tools that will make it easy for you to learn.

Vocabulary

You already know many Spanish words. With just a little bit of attention you can know hundreds more! Let's start with the easiest ones. The following English words have the same meaning and spelling in Spanish:

regular	*doctor*	*total*
vulgar	*actor*	*general*
similar	*tractor*	*local*
singular		

You will quickly think of other words similar to English. I want to increase your interest and motivation by incorporating into your vocabulary many other Spanish words that require no special effort.

English and Spanish have many other look-alikes that differ only in their endings. Here is a summary.

Spanish Word Ending	English Ending	Example in Spanish
al	al	*total, general, local*
or	or	*doctor, actor*
ar	ar	*regular, vulgar*
ible	ible	*posible, terrible*
able	able	*probable, venerable*
sión	sion	*posesión, repulsión*
ción	tion	*reputación, educación*
dad	ty	*ciudad, variedad*
tad	ty	*libertad*

Spanish Word Ending	English Ending	Example in Spanish
mente	ly	*absolutamente*
rio, ria	ry	*canario, ordinario*
oso, osa	ous	*religioso, curioso*
ura	ure	*signatura, lectura*
ina	ine	*gasolina, aspirina*
encio, encia	ence ent,	*experiencia*
ente, ante	ant	*patente, instante*
ivo, iva	ive	*repulsivo, positivo*
uto, ido	ute, ite	*minuto, indefenido*
ucto	uct	*producto, acueducto*
ecto	ect	*defecto, perfecto*
icio, icia	ice, ace	*servicio, palacio*
ico, ica	ic	*música, público*
ema	em	*problema, emblema*
ama	am	*programa, telegrama*

You can easily and quickly expand your Spanish vocabulary by thinking of English words with the endings shown above and converting them into correct Spanish spelling. Spelling is easy because almost everything is spelled as it sounds. They don't have to hold spelling bees in Spanish-speaking countries!

In addition, there are many words that are almost look-alikes. One common pattern is that "qu" often changes to *cu*. "Quarter" becomes *cuarto*, and "question" becomes *cuestión*. Another is that English words beginning with *s* often have Spanish counterparts beginning with *es*. For example: *estudio*, *espléndido*, *especial*. Also, many verb *roots* are also the same: *admirar, mover, dividir*. Always look for the English in the Spanish.

Another approach to expanding your vocabulary is to select ten words or phrases in English for which you want to learn the Spanish and write them down with the Spanish word opposite each. Memorize the list using Memory Blueprint 3 (Rhyming Words), developing visual images that link the cue word to the Spanish. For instance, the cue rhyming word for number 1 is *gun*; if the first Spanish word you want to remember is *si* (meaning "yes," pronounced *see*), you might think, "I pulled a gun to **SEE** if he would say *yes*."

Here's a list of ten words you might choose. Can you think of linking images for them?

		English	Spanish	Pronunciation
1	(Gun)	*yes*	*si*	"see"
2	(Shoe)	*no*	*no*	very short "o"
3	(Tree)	*please*	*por favor*	"por-fah-vor"
4	(Door)	*thank you*	*gracias*	"grah-see-ahs"
5	(Dive)	*how much?*	*cuanto*	"quahnt-oh"
6	(Sticks)	*too much*	*demasiado*	"deh-mah-see-ah-doh"
7	(Heaven)	*food*	*comida*	"coh-mi-dah"
8	(Gate)	*water*	*agua*	"ah-gwah"
9	(Wine)	*bed*	*cama*	"cah-mah"
10	(Hen)	*go away*	*va*	"vah"

Review this three times a day for a couple of days. Then take another list of ten words or phrases and do the same with them.

The next very important step is to tape record the English words or phrases with a pause before speaking each Spanish word or phrase. (A little later on, I'll have some suggestions for learning correct pronunciation.) This will provide you with a cumulative review of what you have learned. You should be able to put hundreds of words on a one-hour tape.

It's helpful to visualize the action that goes with the word you're learning. For instance, if you are learning the word for "ask," imagine yourself asking for something. If you're learning the word for "bed," visualize your bed. If it's the word for "breakfast," see yourself at breakfast. This action of seeing the words in a familiar setting will speed learning and cement them into your permanent vocabulary.

Using Memory Bridges

Memory bridges are especially easy to use with Spanish because there are so many sounds that have meaning in English. Here are three examples. Can you remember the phrase "live without sin"? If so, you have remembered the Spanish word for "without": *sin*, pronounced "seen."

How about "Oh ho, what an eye!" The Spanish word for "eye" is *ojo*, pronounced "oh-ho." And then there is *de repente*, which looks as if it means to "repent," but is actually the word for "suddenly." My bridge: I **REPENT**ed *suddenly*. My bridges make words memorable *to me*. Your bridges will be highly individual and memorable to you.

A woman who had just acquired a Spanish-speaking son-in-law asked me how to remember the greeting *Como esta usted?* ("How are you?"). I said, "Repeat after me: Perry **COMO** is **A STAR** and **YOU SAID** it." That gave her a pattern to build on. She modified the sounds for proper pronunciation, and her new son-in-law was appropriately impressed!

Idioms

Idioms are an interesting challenge because they are not literal translations. In English we say, "He is a go-getter." A Spanish-speaking person who wants to convey the same idea would use a phrase that when literally translated into English means "a wild beast." When dealing with idioms, you must learn a complete phrase and think of its idiomatic equivalent in English, not the individual words in a literal sense.

I recommend that you look over the list of idioms in the excellent University of Chicago Spanish dictionary and select the ones you are most likely to use. Proceed as you did with vocabulary words, learning ten at a time.

Remembering Correct Pronunciation

Up to now you've been learning through reading and other visual study. But a very important part of learning a foreign language is being able to pronounce properly those words you do use. All your work of memorizing the key phrases will be wasted if people can't understand you!

To teach yourself good pronunciation, I highly recommend two tapes from the Crown Publishing *Complete Living Language*™ series. Both start by providing a complete, accurate, and easily grasped key to correct pronunciation of every letter with a unique method: Repeat and play back, repeat and play back—it's the only way for the sounds to become second nature.

The Crown tapes use what we might call standard pronunciation, but you should know that the same words can have different pronunciations—and quite different meanings—in different Spanish-speaking areas. It's rather like different regional accents

in the United States—only more so. Sometimes the pronunciation is so different that a word that is very proper in one country
becomes vulgar in another. So you might want to invest in a
book that lists language variations by country.

The Secret of Memorizing From Cassettes

There are two steps in learning another language. The first is
being able to speak it yourself. The second is the ability to understand when another person is speaking it. Maybe you've heard
the ads for the cassette courses: "Just listen and repeat." That
takes care of *your* ability to speak it. But if you expect to be able
to understand a person whose native tongue is Spanish, you
must be able to remember what a sentence or phrase sounds like
at a higher speed.

You can do this by practicing with a cassette, listening to one
phrase at a time. Stop the tape and learn to pronounce each
phrase slowly and accurately. Then try to repeat it ten times,
increasing the speed each time. You won't have to talk that fast,
but you will have to *listen* that fast! This is a major breakthrough
in remembering phrases the way you will probably hear them
spoken. So no matter how slow your repetition is at first, do it
accurately.

My friend Mort Herold, who taught accordion before becoming a great memory expert, says, "Never let them practice anything the wrong way."

If You Want to Learn the Grammar

The Crown tapes and accompanying books provide all you need
to study verb tenses and other rules of grammar. Then you can
use Memory Blueprint 2 (Spaces Around Your Body) to line up
and memorize each tense, probably at the rate of one tense every
three days. For example, take the six uses of the present tense:

1. To your left put "I speak Spanish." (Action or present state)
2. In front, place "I speak Spanish every day." (A habitual
   action)
3. To your right, put "Think before you speak." (A general
   truth)
4. Behind you, "He speaks wildly." (Vividness in the past)

5. Under your feet, "I'll be speaking tomorrow." (Near future)
6. On your head, "I've been speaking for four hours." (Action in the past that continues to the present)

The subjunctive has a lot of rules, and is one of the hardest parts of Spanish grammar to learn because it is used only with certain words. This is a great place to use Memory Blueprint 1 (Initial Letters). Build memory joggers based on the initial letters of the words that take the subjunctive—in either Spanish or English. For example, the subjunctive ending is used after a verb expressing

D oubt

J oy

F ear

H ope

S orrow

My first memory jogger is: **DJ** (disk jockey) at **FHS** (Foxboro High School).

The subjunctive is used after verbs expressing:

D oubt
R egret
I mportance

P ossibility
U rgency
N ecessity

My memory jogger was **DRI PUN**. The emotions were not expressed in that order, but they don't have to be remembered in the order given in the textbook.

I use another memory jogger, **VINN**, to remember that the subjunctive follows something Vague, Indefinite, Negative, or Nonexistent.

The verbs in Spanish end in *-ar*, *-er*, and, *-ir*. These are the three conjugation endings. Each conjugation also has different endings to express each tense. I would suggest you construct a chart showing the endings for each conjugation and each tense.

That will enable you to see what endings are the same for all conjugations. Learning them is a matter of creating blueprints and using a lot of rote repetition. If you select a regular verb, you can use a seven-point blueprint, such as 2, 3, or 4, to learn to conjugate the seven principle tenses of that verb. I try to go through a representative of each complete conjugation daily.

Walking Right In to Rote Repetition

Learning numbers, the alphabet, the conjugations of verbs, the days of the week, and months of the year can be helped through rhythmic repetition. I found that this worked best for me by learning in rhythm to my footsteps. At first I could only say the words with every other step, but practice brought me to the point of being able to hit every step—about 120 to the minute!

Building—and keeping—a large vocabulary is like eating: one meal at a time, one mouthful at a time—and always well chewed.

A Final Word

Beyond mere memory I see before me the possibilities of a tremendous development of the mind by the revolutionary use of simple methods that will vastly increase the ability to store pertinent, useful, productive knowledge in the dependable available body of thought—the permanent memory—and that will also provide the time in which to do it.

Permit me to close with a few lines from the English poet, Thomas Watson.

> The thirst to know and understand—
> A large and liberal discontent:
> These are the goods in life's rich hand
> The things that are most excellent.

Index